C000134165

Stay Smart!

Smart things to know about... is a complete library of the world's smartest business ideas. **Smart** books put you on the inside track to the knowledge and skills that make the most successful people tick.

Each book brings you right up to speed on a crucial business issue. The subjects that business people tell us they most want to master are:

*Smart Things to Know about **Brands & Branding**,* JOHN MARIOTTI

*Smart Things to Know about **Business Finance**,* KEN LANGDON

*Smart Things to Know about **Change**,* DAVID FIRTH

*Smart Things to Know about **Customers**,* ROS JAY

*Smart Things to Know about **E-Commerce**,* MIKE CUNNINGHAM

*Smart Things to Know about **Knowledge Management**,*
TOM M. KOULOPOULOS & CARL FRAPPAOLO

*Smart Things to Know about **Strategy**,* RICHARD KOCH

*Smart Things to Know about **Teams**,* ANNEMARIE CARACCIOLO

You can stay **Smart** by e-mailing us at **capstone_publishing@msn.com**. Let us keep you up to date with new Smart books, Smart updates, a Smart newsletter and Smart seminars and conferences. Get in touch to discuss your needs.

CAPSTONE

Smart

THINGS TO KNOW ABOUT

Knowledge
Management

THOMAS M. KOULOPOULOS

CARL FRAPPAOLO

Copyright © Thomas M. Koulopoulos and Carl Frappaolo 1999

The right of Thomas M. Koulopoulos and Carl Frappaolo to be identified as the authors of this work has been asserted in accordance with the Copyright, Designs and Patents Act 1988

First published 1999 by

Capstone US
Business Books Network
163 Central Avenue
Suite 2
Hopkins Professional Building
Dover
NH 03820
USA

Capstone Publishing Limited
Oxford Centre for Innovation
Mill Street
Oxford OX2 0JX
United Kingdom
http://www.capstone.co.uk

CIP catalogue records for this book are available from the British Library and the US Library of Congress

ISBN 1-84112-041-3

Typeset in 11/15 pt Sabon by
Sparks Computer Solutions Ltd, Oxford
http://www.sparks.co.uk
Printed and bound by
T.J. International Ltd, Padstow, Cornwall

This book is printed on acid-free paper

Substantial discounts on bulk quantities of Capstone books are available to corporations, professional associations and other organizations. If you are in the USA or Canada, phone the LPC Group for details on (1-800-626-4330) or fax (1-800-243-0138). Everywhere else, phone Capstone Publishing on (+44-1865-798623) or fax (+44-1865-240941).

TK
To Anastasios,
In whose eyes I see all I need to know.

CF
To Theresa and Teresa, my alpha and omega.

Contents

What is Smart?

The *Smart* series is a new way of learning. *Smart* books will improve your understanding and performance in some of the critical areas you face today like *customers, strategy, change, e-commerce, brands, influencing skills, knowledge management, finance, teamworking, partnerships*.

Smart books summarize accumulated wisdom as well as providing original cutting-edge ideas and tools that will take you out of theory and into action.

The widely respected business guru Chris Argyris points out that even the most intelligent individuals can become ineffective in organizations. Why? Because we are so busy working that we fail to learn about ourselves. We stop reflecting on the changes around us. We get sucked into the patterns of behavior that have produced success for us in the past, not realizing that it may no longer be appropriate for us in the fast-approaching future.

There are three ways the *Smart* series helps prevent this happening to you:

- by increasing your self-awareness

- by developing your understanding, attitude and behavior

- by giving you the tools to challenge the status quo that exists in your organization.

Smart people need smart organizations. You could spend a third of your career hopping around in search of the Holy Grail, or you could begin to create your own smart organization around you today.

Finally a reminder that books don't change the world, people do. And although the *Smart* series offers you the brightest wisdom from the best practitioners and thinkers, these books throw the responsibility on you to *apply* what you're learning in your work.

Because the truly smart person knows that reading a book is the start of the process and not the end ...

As Eric Hoffer says, "In times of change, learners inherit the world, while the learned remain beautifully equipped to deal with a world that no longer exists."

David Firth
Smartmaster

Acknowledgments

Authors often quip that they hate to write but love to have written. Although there may be precious few individuals who enjoy the tedious nature of writing, the fact remains that to hold your own completed book in your hands is the greatest reward for any author. Although that moment may be a very personal one, no book or author stands alone and our first compulsion and obligation upon finishing *Smart Things to Know about Knowledge Management* is to recognize the many contributors to this effort.

Smart Things to Know about Knowledge Management is a project to which many smart people contributed. We, as authors, had the benefit of their company, wisdom and support. The credit for any success this book achieves is shared with these fine people whose names and contributions we feebly attempt to acknowledge in the space of these short pages, with the keen understanding that our debt to them is far greater than a few paragraphs can ever convey.

The Delphi team must be at the top of this list for providing specific contributions and the context of a global team of thought leaders - the likes of which comes along only once in a very great while. Thanks to Nick, Mary Ann, Carlene, Dan, John, Andrea, Linda, Jacqueline, Rich, Tom Reed, Pat, Debby and Margie as well as those individuals who made specific contributions to the book, including: Nathaniel, for the discussion on incentivization in Chapter Four; Hadley; for much of the early research in Delphi's knowledge management efforts; Mark, for the Bastille case study; Stacie, for much of the material on knowledge leadership in Chapter Five; Wayne, for assisting in developing the concept of Corporate Instinct; and our assistant Jeanne, for keeping our lives sane – sometimes at the price of her own sanity.

In addition, thanks to the principals of our dedicated international partners who represent Delphi around the world and have been a source of ideas, inspiration, and pride for us as they bring their own experiences back from around the globe: Jeff and Ced in Australia; Hiroshi and Hiroyuki in Japan; Jose and Laura in South America; John and Bryan in Canada.

Our own best education constantly comes from the many clients, seminar and conference attendees who form our extended community of thought leaders. Included among these are: Janice Scites at AT&T; Chuck Seeley at Warner Lambert; Dr Seymour Siegel at Pfizer; Kathy Hagen; Jan Daley, Dan Holtshouse and the entire team at Xerox; Michael Berens at AARP; Alden Globe at JD Edwards; Fernando Vellanoweth at the State of California; Keith Davidson of Xplor International; Dave Snowden of IBM; Atul Aneja at Intel who originally introduced us to the stimulus/response matrix in Chapter Two; Brad Meyer of Collaboration Ltd; Rob Patzig; David Watkins, Brian Plotkin, Charlie Gray and Suzanne Fickes for their help in the Bastille case study; Timothy M. Hickernell at Commonwealth Edison; Thomas Brailsford at Hallmark Cards; Jim Allen of Dow Chemical; Kent Greens at British Petroleum.

Our efforts have also been influenced heavily by the luminary personalities and the *Delphi Company of Fellows* that we have had the good fortune to know: Peter Drucker, Paul Romer, Bob Buckman, Hubert Saint-Onge, and Paul Strassmann; and of course the many authors whose ideas and insights we have liberally sprinkled throughout the book as "Smart quotes" and "Smart people to have on your side."

Then there is our agent, John Willig, who, although we admit some bias, has to be one of the most tenacious, professional, and supportive literary agents in the industry. Rumor has it that John's mom, a well-respected figure in the publishing community, raised him with his nose deeply embedded in books. We are clearly the beneficiaries of his wealth of tacit knowledge.

Needless to say that all of these efforts would not have amounted to a book were it not for the smart folks at Capstone, especially Mark Allin. Capstone's savvy, speed, and style reflect many of the innovative traits and competitive attitudes we discuss in the book.

Finally, the greatest thanks go to our families: our wives Ann and Debbie; mothers and fathers Theresa and Charles, Michael and Maria; brothers and sisters Nick, Bob and Colette. Their unwavering support has been the foundation of our inspiration. And then of course there are our children Anna, Mia, Teresa and Anastasios, who are the very essence of our life's work. At the end of the day it is in their eyes that we see all of the smart lessons we have learned and taught – and through their eyes will it be judged just how smart we really were.

Introduction

A Smart History of the Modern Enterprise

Two hundred years in the making, the Industrial Revolution is being turned on its ear. Concepts that were central to the formation of organizations, employment, and work itself are being challenged as a new breed of Smart managers leverage knowledge to make unparalleled advances in their ability to innovate, compete and connect with their customers.

By the middle of the 20th century, American business culture was marked by very high levels of bureaucratization, organizational segmentation, and impersonalized – indeed, depersonalized – environments. Hordes of writers and social scientists warned that the average worker, whether blue- or white-collar, felt trapped in stultifying jobs, toiling away only because there were bills to pay and mortgages to be met. Books chronicling this alienation, especially William Allan Whyte's *The Organization Man* and Sloan Wilson's *The Man in the Gray Flannel Suit* were bestsellers in the 1950s.

At the same time, the nations of Europe – and especially Asia – had recovered from their total devastation and were becoming important players in the world market. More importantly, many of these new enterprises were doing things differently. Their employees were more involved in planning how to do their jobs, management and labor worked together, and an obsession with quality went beyond sloganeering. Americans began to hear stories of Japanese workers gathering before the workday to exercise and sing company songs.

The market share held by American companies in many industries – steel, electronics, automobiles, shipbuilding, to name but a few – was shrinking. Moreover, there was a sense that most companies just didn't work; they were inefficient, fragmented, and resistant to new ideas.

What had started as a very smart way to run a company soon became the ball and chain of American industry.

Then, in 1982, two relatively unknown management consultants, Thomas J. Peters and Robert H. Waterman, Jr. published *In Search of Excellence: Lessons from America's Best-Run Companies*, which pointed out that those organizations thriving in a brutally competitive environment seemed to share a set of common values and practices, despite their wide variations in size, mission, product, and customer base.

In 1992 Michael Hammer and James Champy published *Reengineering the Corporation*, their manifesto for a reengineering revolution. The crisis was so desperate that only "obliteration" seemed an adequate antidote for the American corporation, according to Hammer and Champy. They were right, but they provided only the wake-up call. So much of this was dogma and charismatic "vision-building." CEOs and stockholders bought into the charisma, and short-term gains resulted as quality and reengineering movements raced through corporations. Hatchets came down *en masse* on the front office workers.

Still the pathology of industrialization remained. Not because people lacked the desire to change, but rather because the tools for effecting changes were still embryonic. The technology, communications, and methods of the industrial era continued to loom over corporate infrastructure and culture.

And so it is with this very brief – and admittedly selective – history of the evolution of the modern, industrial business environment, that we are now turning to the knowledge-based enterprise and the core competency for survival – *knowledge management.*

Indeed, the smart manager instinctively turns to knowledge management at this time. The smart manager sees knowledge management as a way to nurture and promote that which represents the delta between an organization's book value and its market value.

In a knowledge-based economy, knowledge management is the critical element of a business strategy that will allow the organization to accelerate the rate at which it handles new market challenges and opportunities, and it does so by leveraging its most precious of resources, collective know-how, talent and experience.

But, a smart manager also realizes that knowledge management is not a simple issue. It is not a technology, although technology should be positioned to facilitate it. It is not a directive, although strategic leadership is imperative. It is not a business strategy, although one aligned with the tenets of knowledge management must exist. The smart manager must put all these in place, but also build a culture that promotes faith in collectively sharing and thinking.

Knowledge management tells us that we should take stock in our greatest, most precious organizational asset, intellectual capital.

The smart manger understands that his organization must challenge age-old adages, no longer rely on core products but core competencies.

In short, the smart manager understands that in today's environment, knowledge management is the only hope for growing and responding at a pace whose benchmark is constantly exceeding everyone's wildest expectations.

But, where to begin? Claims of knowledge management's promise abound in terms of its potential for building a new era of organizational value. And the solutions and technologies that can be applied to manage knowledge are following in close pursuit.

Yet knowledge management is plagued by hype and confusion. The field is vast and poorly defined. There are few well-established benchmarks for its measurement or implementation. (But, then again, the same could have been said of the factories of the nineteenth century.) Unfortunately most of us don't have the patience to wait another two centuries for the answers.

No wonder so many of you want to scream "stop all the noise, give me the facts."

It is in answer to your call that this book was written.

The book is written from a practical point of view. Too much of the attention focused on knowledge management takes the form of theorizing and discussion. While this may be interesting and valuable to the world of academia, you, as a smart manager, need to know why increasing numbers of companies have moved beyond academic discussion, and are taking concrete steps towards developing a corporate knowledge management solution. You need to appreciate the benefits they are realizing from this move. You need to know which technologies are providing the fuel that propels an organization into the field of knowledge management.

You want smart answers to questions such as: What is knowledge management? How can it help my company? Is knowledge management a business imperative of the 21st century? How is knowledge management implemented? What type of changes and education does it require? Knowing the answers to these questions is characteristic of a smart manager. These are the questions that this book will answer.

But brace yourself. Answering these questions is not a simple task. Knowledge management is not a single-threaded issue. Knowledge management mandates consideration and appreciation for the business imperative that gave way to knowledge management, the technologies that have mandated knowledge driven economies, the technologies that facilitate knowledge management, establishment of new business procedures, and the creation of new corporate structures.

This book introduces you to these many facets of knowledge management and provides an education that promotes self-sufficiency in addressing, discussing and utilizing the powers of knowledge management in a competent manner. It comprises six chapters and a glossary, each focusing on a different facet of this subject. You are encouraged to begin your education by honing in on those areas of greatest interest to you, prior to a second complete reading.

A smart overview of this book

Chapter 1 – Fuel for Innovation

This chapter lays the business foundation for why knowledge management has become imperative. It builds a case for the economic, social, and business factors driving the adoption and appeal of knowledge management. It focuses on issues such as the shift in wealth creation from hard goods to intellect, the accelerating speed of innovation, and the competitive advantage of knowledge sharing. It also introduces and discusses contrarian views raised to dismiss the value of knowledge management. This chapter helps you answer the question, "Why knowledge management?"

Chapter 2 – Cornerstones of Knowledge

Building on the business imperative for knowledge management, this chapter provides you with a review of the origins and foundation of knowledge management. The philosophical basis for knowledge management is introduced, with a focus on the cornerstone ideas that have shaped modern thinking on the subject. Key individuals and pioneers in the field such as Polanyi, Nonaka, Senge *et al.* are introduced. It is here that you will get a clear definition of knowledge management. We provide frameworks to help you visualize and explain the benefits of knowledge management.

Chapter 3 – Knoware: The Technology of Knowledge Management

You must appreciate that knowledge management is not a technology, or even a class of technologies. Nonetheless, many of the reasons reinforcing the need for knowledge management are driven by technology (e.g. Internet, workflow). Moreover, a smart manager realizes that the practices of knowledge management can be augmented and facilitated through the application of technology. But with so many technology claims, where do you focus your attention? How do you separate the hype from reality, and map the needs of your organization to myriad technology choices? Here are your smart answers to these questions. This chapter maps available technologies to the applications of knowledge management, utilizing enough detail to make you competent in understanding the role of – and discussing the benefits of – technology to a knowledge-driven initiative, without getting mired in technical detail.

Chapter 4 – The Softer Side of Knowledge Management

If you understand only one thing about knowledge management, it should be this: the heart of knowledge management rests in the cultural practices and organizational attitudes regarding collaboration, knowledge sharing and open communication. This chapter provides you with a definitive list of the litany of cultural issues that the smart manager will confront head-on in order to ensure his/her organization's success in the knowledge-economy age. You are given advice on how to address issues such as the ownership of knowledge, how to build a knowledge-sharing culture and how to establish compensation programs that give incentives to a learning organization.

Chapter 5 – Leading the Knowledge-based Organization

Who is the smart manager of knowledge? Is it the CKO? This chapter focuses on the leadership requirements for a knowledge initiative. You receive insight on how to identify the most appropriate personnel to assume the role of the knowledge leader, and how best to position this individual(s) within the corporate structure.

Chapter 6 – What We Don't Know

Last, as every smart manager knows, survival is more than just dealing with the realities of today, it is anticipating and planning for the future. This chapter concludes your education with insights into where knowledge management might lead us. It provides a glimpse into the next 5–20 years, with a practical assessment of the initial stages in the evolution of knowledge-based organizations. You gain the perspective needed to develop a sound strategy beyond the planning horizon, and into the knowledge-based organization of the new millennium. Now that's smart!

1

Fuel for Innovation

As every smart manager knows, the merits of a new business metaphor and/or technology genre must be judged in terms of a business case. No surprise then that we begin by doing just that, developing the business case for knowledge management.

On the heels of several other business models (fads?) that have come and gone with varying degrees of success, you must ask yourself, "Is knowledge management just another fad to keep consultants and authors in business?" It's a valid question.

It helps to understand that the knowledge management movement is hardly new, certainly not when measured by the yardstick of recent management movements, whose typical lifecycle rarely pushes a decade of mainstream popularity.

They copied all that they could follow but they couldn't copy my mind, and I left 'em sweating and stealing a year and a half behind.

Rudyard Kipling

Knowledge management's contemporary roots (we will ignore its origins in epistemology – the study of knowledge) date back to the mid twentieth century, when the first wave of post-World-War-II college graduates reached the work force. Funded by the heavy investment of the GI Bill, and the enormous collection of wartime scientific discovery, this newly minted workforce had an edge unlike any other generation – higher education. The steady incline in educated workers and the coincident increase in institutions of higher education created a steamroller that may well account for the singular most compelling need for knowledge management. Certainly it was the genesis of the modern-day knowledge economy.

Today the knowledge economy is not only built on the obvious need to manage the enormous intellectual capital, generated by this legacy, but also the demands created by an ever-decreasing half-life of intellectual residency – the time any one knowledge worker stays on any single job.

By the mid 1990s, smart managers began to recognize knowledge as the key differentiating factor for their organizations. You had lived through reengineering, TQM, and strategic management initiatives and began to realize that traditional differentiators such as "quality" had a place in the organization, but they were no longer going to drive competitiveness. Parity had been reached in the back room. The smart manager realized that innovation was quickly turning into the core competitive mandate.

But as a smart manager you already recognize how technology has crumbled the barriers erected by traditional competitive ingredients. You recognize how developing companies have been enabled to provide the base ingredients of quality, and customer support, as well as, if not better than, established industrial giants.

You recognize that the companies that are most successful are the ones that continue to provide personalized solutions to customers, with the highest quality, at the lowest price. These companies assume that their competitors will always be able to emulate what they do over time. The smart manager knows that the key to success today is measured in an organization's ability to maintain innovation, to continuously set the industry benchmark.

Where killer products may once have enjoyed market cycles that spanned generations, today, such products may only enjoy their day in the sun for a period of months. It is this focus on constant change and creativity that dramatically separates knowledge management from previous business paradigms, such as reengineering, that relied on established constant processes.

Little wonder that the world's attention has shifted to the knowledge that exists in corporations, and on ways in which that knowledge can be nurtured, used and re-used most effectively.

KILLER QUESTIONS

Do you survive on your core competencies or core products?

The end of reengineering

To appreciate the value of knowledge management, it is actually helpful to compare it with what may well be the final throws of the industrial age: reengineering.

For many smart managers, the springboard for knowledge management was the painful realization that their organizations came together as the result of the massive reengineering initiatives that swept the business world over the past decade.

When an industry or a company begins to experience change, the age-old rules that ensured success for so long seem insufficient to stop a gradual slide in profitability. The past becomes less and less a mirror for the future, and corporate memory, or established rules and procedures of operation begin to lose their luster.

Painfully aware that there was discontinuity between the market environment and an organization's learned response, many managers initiated radical reengineering initiatives, destroying the implicit repositories of their corporate memory, and rebuilding processes and strategies to address the new environment.

While reengineering served to rejuvenate these companies, many made a fatal mistake – they replaced an outdated, invalid corporate memory with a new, soon-to-be invalid corporate memory. Reengineering assumed that a single one-time fix to a situation was the answer. Reengineering mentalities created vicious cycles, in which solutions soon became new problems. *Why?* Reengineering fails to take into consideration the ongoing and rapid change that characterizes today's markets.

KILLER QUESTIONS

Are you your own fiercest competitor?

But, as a smart manager, you know that organizations do not have the luxury of resting on their laurels. Once mighty giants of the past have become extinct in the face of a radically changing environment, deposed by smaller, nimbler, smarter competitors. You recognize that your organization is constantly challenged by new competitors, new customer demands and new markets.

You know that organizational strength does not come from knowledge of what has worked in the past, but in the ability to continuously regenerate and repurpose the knowledge of an organization, its processes and its markets. Smart managers who underwent reengineering realized that they needed to put in place mechanisms by which their organization could break free from the shackles of corporate memory. Smart managers have come to realize that reengineering provides a short-term fix, at best. But because

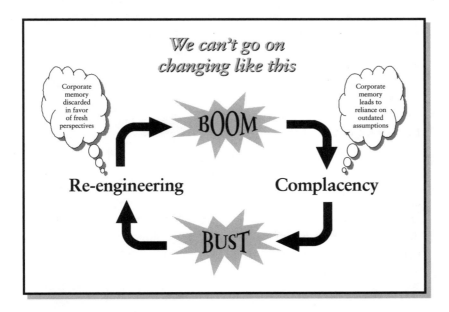

it assumes that the market conditions it addressed would not change, it soon creates a memory of how things were, and out-dated products and procedures. A smart manager ensures reengineering efforts will not need to be repeated every time the company is brought to the brink of collapsing under the weight of the past. And, the smart manager recognizes that this is the domain of knowledge management.

Unlike reengineering, knowledge management assumes a constant vigilance, encourages constant modification and innovation – at a rate that at least keeps pace with changing market dynamics. The smart manager recognizes that in today's market, change is inevitable, and therefore innovation must be constant. You recognize that the fuel for innovation is the organization's knowledge base. And, you appreciate the fragile and volatile asset that knowledge is. You know that in order to remain competitive, you must harvest the knowledge of the past and build on it to respond to the market of tomorrow.

Learning to forget

It is not easy to put these concepts into practice. In addition to the very real technology challenges of capturing and sharing knowledge, there are undeniable cultural issues, which rock many firmly-held assumptions regarding competitiveness and personnel development to their core. Indeed, the overwhelming effect of this new market dynamic is a result of the fact that it is changing some of the most basic tenets by which we behave and make decisions.

> Romer is widely recognised as author and architect of new growth theory. This theory positions innovation and creativity at the fulcrum of economic growth. It proposes that in an advanced economy, the most important policies may be the ones that influence the rate of technological innovation in the private sector. Professor Romer's theories have been widely covered in the business press, and last year he was named one of America's 25 most influential people by *Time* magazine.

Since childhood we are all taught not to repeat the mistakes of the past. History is a vast series of lessons learned and we ignore them at our peril, so we are told. But what if we challenge the generality of that belief? What if our memories were distinct from our history? Might it be that, as with so many generalizations, we have lost the essence of truth by using too broad a brush to paint the parable? We are treading on sacred turf here, but doubt that we are alone.

Take a moment and consider that knowledge is like radioactive isotopes – it decays at various rates based on its composition. Some knowledge has a half-life of days, while other forms of knowledge will endure for eons. For example, the knowledge applied to popular fashion is clearly short-lived. We all laugh at how silly we look in the clothes we thought so stylish in pictures taken just ten years ago. On the other hand, the knowledge gained from the great democratic experiments of ancient Athens still applies in our modern-day forms of government. Our notion of democracy has changed and will continue to change, but is still based upon and relevant to tenets that emanated centuries ago.

As a smart manager, think of knowledge and its relationship to memory as a whirlpool. Items of knowledge that have fleeting value reside at the vor-

KILLER QUESTIONS

Do you value acquisition of new knowledge over the creation of structure and standards?

tex, constantly being sucked down and recycled. However, static principles, that help to define the context of our interactions as a society, reside on the periphery, moving rapidly, but remaining intact for a period of time. The question now becomes, "should we use the same benchmark for both of these events, and all of those in-between the two extremes, to govern our actions in the future?" Clearly not.

Why do the ranks of the F500 change so often? Organizational strength does not come from knowledge of what has worked in the past, but the ability to regenerate knowledge of the organization, its processes and its markets. Smart managers realize that knowledge management is the antithesis of the crisis-driven mentality of reengineering. Knowledge management assumes a constant vigilance of change, and encourages constant modification – innovation – at a rate that at least keeps pace with changing market dynamics.

Make no mistake here, knowledge management emphasizes the re-use of previous experiences and practices, but its focus is on mapping these to the changing landscape of the market. If that sounds simple, then try answering the following question, "What is your organization's core competency?" If you answered with a product name, you're shackled by the past. The chances are, if you answered in this manner, you are referring to a most successful product. Success forms the most restrictive shackles. Your competency must outlive product success. Products should exist at the vortex of the whirlpool – constantly changing. Your core competencies should live at the outer limits of the whirlpool.

Because things are speeding up so fast, your competitive advantage is your ability to use quickly what you've discovered and to continually improve on it and move beyond it, because somebody's going to be copying it, and fast.

Dan Holtshouse (Director of business strategy and knowledge initiatives, Xerox)

The smart organization has reached the stage where its knowledge of the past plays less of a role in guiding its future than its understanding of current circumstances and an innate ability to process and respond to these circumstances. The smart organization makes a subtle yet profound shift – from relying on its "experience" (or knowledge of the past), to relying on its "competencies" (or resourcefulness to handle the future). Knowledge of the past is only valuable inasmuch as it provides a perspective on the future. Competency, on the other hand, equips the organization to respond to as yet unknown forces for change.

Still believe that the past is sacred turf? Take heart. Ultimately it's all generational. There is a whole new generation of wired kids (the smart managers of tomorrow) who are going to regard the way we make decisions today in as anathema. We wonder how we are going to survive at this pace of change - they will not even question it.

Innovation as key

Clearly, there is growing realization that knowledge and the ability to continuously innovate are factors of production, like land and capital, and that there should be a way to optimize them. But knowledge is a human function. It originates and resides in a human being. In that sense, it is a misnomer to say that we can manage knowledge. We cannot manage what happens in people's brains, and it's presumptuous to say we can manage people's thought processes. So then is knowledge management a fool's dream? No, the smart manager realizes that the goal for knowledge management is not controlling people's thoughts, but focuses on ways to manage how that knowledge is used, and to build systems and mechanisms to facilitate the expression and thereby sharing of ideas and know-how. This is the concept behind one of the most important frameworks for understanding the benefits and challenges of knowledge management – the knowledge chain and return on time.

The knowledge chain

As a smart manager, you must be able to understand and articulate why competitive advantage is not only the sum of the intellectual parts of an enterprise; it is the speed of summation, which we refer to as *return on time*.

As the pace of innovation, mergers and partnerships, and obsolescence increases, the speed of your company's knowledge chain becomes a bench-

ACQUIRING KNOWLEDGE: USING KNOWLEDGE MANAGEMENT FOR SMART MERGERS AND ACQUISITIONS

One of the greatest opportunities for the application of knowledge management may be that of facilitating mergers and acquisitions – an area of extensive activity lately, but fraught with risk and cost.

Enhancing a company's knowledge chain often means going outside and acquiring knowledge. But integrating a new company into an existing culture can slow the knowledge chain more than any other activity. Imagine the consequence of monthly acquisitions and you have a sense for the challenge Platinum Technology faced.

Several years ago, Platinum Technology, an organization specializing in software and IT services made a strategic business decision to grow the organization through an aggressive acquisition plan. Indeed, in less than six years, Platinum acquired over 60 companies. In formulating this plan, management was smart enough to realize that part of an acquisition involved the assumption of intellectual assets, including the knowledge of the products of the acquired company, how they are marketed, how they are sold, current customers, etc. If this knowledge could be effectively integrated into the established Platinum knowledgebase, it was presumed that revenues from the acquired company could be readily absorbed and continued with existing Platinum sales staff.

In 1997, Platinum Technology undertook the task of developing and implementing an enterprise-wide knowledge sharing system for its entire base of 1,800 sales and marketing professionals. Its primary application is supporting the acquisition strategy.

Once an acquisition is announced, knowledge about the acquisition itself and knowledge regarding the target company is placed in the mergers and acquisitions on-line knowledge base. Via user profiles, this information is immediately pushed to interested parties within Platinum. By sharing this knowledge across the enterprise, especially with the Platinum sales force, it is estimated that sales people save two hours per week, and other Platinum professionals one hour trying to become acclimated to the new company and its products. As a result, the Platinum sales force moves forward with the acquired product lines in real-time and Platinum purports a $6,000,000 return on a $750,000 knowledge management investment.

mark challenge for leveraging its intellectual capital into
success. When considering the need for and potential
impact of knowledge management to an organization,
the smart manager thinks in terms of the knowledge
chain.

Knowledge management depends less on the amount of
information than on the number of connections that link
information and people. The dynamic linking aspect of
knowledge is a critical distinguishing factor between
knowledge management and information management.
It is the navigation between information and people
throughout a value chain of activities that constitutes a knowledge chain.

There are four steps in the knowledge chain that determine the uniqueness
and longevity of any organization. They are also the factors that allow a
smart organization to innovate or change successfully, while extinction
claims its competitors. These four steps are:

- internal awareness

- internal responsiveness

- external responsiveness

- external awareness.

Internal awareness

In its simplest terms, internal awareness is the ability of an organization to

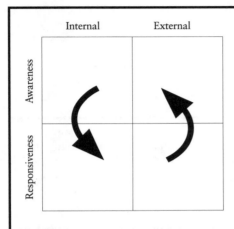

	Internal	External
Awareness		
Responsiveness		

The knowledge chain (K-chain) is a series of interactions that constitute an organization's cycle of innovation. Knowledge management creates permeability between the four cells of the K-chain and accelerates the speed of innovation. The four stages of the knowledge chain define the flow of knowledge through an enterprise, as shown in this illustration.

quickly assess its inventory of skills and core competency. This appears to be a simple task, yet few organizations have mastered it. Consider, for example, what the core competency of your organization is: ask yourself, "Why are we successful?" Again, a smart manager will not respond with a product name, recognizing that this is not a competency, but a temporary market advantage. In today's market, products must be continuously reinvented, with an ever decreasing product lifecycle. It is what Peter Drucker refers to as organized abandonment, the ability to literally cannibalize your greatest successes in order to deliver the next successful product before your competitors.

The smart manager thinks of internal awareness in terms of "What do we do?" as opposed to "What do we make?" For example, an architect's job can be described as either to design buildings or to translate human needs into aesthetically pleasing and functionally responsive structures. It's much

KILLER
QUESTIONS

- How well *do* the individuals in your organization understand the environment external to the organization (e.g. your competition, customers, market dynamics, government regulations, etc.)?
- How well *do* the individuals in your organization understand your organizational environment (e.g. roles and responsibilities, core competencies, talents, etc.)?

easier to say that a residential architect designs ranches or split entries. But what happens to the architect if demand for these types of buildings declines, or even disappears? Competencies always outlive products.

Strong emphasis on functional organization structures that often permeate traditional companies, inhibits the development of internal awareness. Organizations with a rigid functional structure most often define their core competency as their products and services, not their skills. As James Brian Quinn recounts in the Intelligent Enterprise:

Smart quotes

The only irreplaceable capital an organization possess is the knowledge and ability of its people. The productivity of that capital depends on how effectively people share their competence with those who can use it.

Andrew Carnegie

The question usually posed is, "How can we position our products (or product lines) for competitive advantage?" not, "What critical skills should we develop to be best in the world from our customers' viewpoint?" The former builds current profits, the latter builds long-term preeminence.

The smart manager recognizes that it is this long-term preeminence that organizations need most if they are to weather changing markets. But the systems and institutions in place in many organizations undermine this

A SMART APPROACH TO INCENTIVIZATION

Xerox Corporation discovered that their global service technicians exchanged much of what they knew through informal networks. Technicians relied heavily on the face-to-face exchange of war-stories regarding field experience. Although effective in building experience over periods of time, the rapid stream of new products and the distributed nature of the service force did not allow for the luxury of sharing across service teams.

Smart managers seeing this natural phenomenon seized the opportunity to build on this cultural practice and effect it across the entire worldwide staff of Xerox service technicians.

Today, rather than letting the tacit knowledge disseminate haphazardly though "water cooler" conversations, service technicians are encouraged to share their stories by entering them into an on-line system known as Eureka. While it was obvious to managers that this approach would result in increased productivity by wide-scale dissemination of best practices and innovative approaches to problems, the challenge of motivating the service technicians to enter their stories into Eureka, rather than just sharing them verbally, was an issue of significant challenge.

Recognizing that the service technicians took pride in their ability to innovate and respond creatively, an incentivization system was developed not based on financial reward, but on recognition. The authoring service technician's name is attached and prominently displayed with each online tip. In addition, each tip must be peer-reviewed and the reviewer's name is also associated with the posting. The results have been overwhelming. In the first month of availability, over 5,000 tips were entered into Eureka. Now Xerox is looking at ways to productize Eureka for use by other organizations with similar knowledge sharing challenges.

SMART PEOPLE
TO HAVE ON
YOUR SIDE:

PETER
DRUCKER

objective. This is especially true in functional organization structures where, as Quinn notes:

Each functional group has a psychological and political need to see itself as the company's special source of strategic strength. In neither event are there strong incentives to build the cross-divisional corporate skills that would lead to enterprise preeminence. Corporate effectiveness is undercut to satisfy personal or divisional goals.

Smart managers not only offer incentives for building cross-organizational skill sets, they also make the collective whole aware of these skills, thereby creating high levels of internal awareness. Creating this level of awareness is indeed the principal challenge of the smart manager. Once the organization has established its own awareness, it can proceed to the remainder of the Knowledge Chain. Until then it is relying far more on the temporal success of its products than on its core skills and competencies.

Internal responsiveness

A smart manager knows, however, that awareness of an organization's competencies does not guarantee a clear path to successful products or services. An organization may be well aware of its strengths and market demand, yet not be able to adequately effect change within itself quickly enough to meet market requirements. In a study, conducted by the Delphi Group, of 350 respondents, 30% indicated that they had greater external awareness than internal responsiveness. In other words these respondents indicated: "we are better at understanding the market then we are at rallying and coordinating our own resources in response." No wonder 50% of respondents to the same survey indicated that a good idea had more chance of resulting in a new startup or ending up at a competitor before their own organization acted on it.

Internal responsiveness considers how quickly competencies can be translated into actions to bring a product to market or respond to a customer need. It's the ability to respond quickly and seize an opportunity. There's no point in responding quickly, though, if it's too late. Reengineering, for example, is often little more than over-compensation for a company's inability to respond to a series of small market shifts over an extended period. Like a numbed hand placed on a hot stove, such companies may become aware of the extent of the damage only after they smell their own burning flesh. Organizations that can manage their knowledge, on the other hand, are "wired" with high levels of continuous awareness (both external and internal) and perception through all levels and functional areas. This enables them to draw much closer to other parts of themselves and, as a result, closer to the market.

External responsiveness

The smart manager knows that in any organization, and industry, success is ultimately measured by the ability to best meet the requirements of this step in the knowledge chain, external responsiveness. When all is said and done, an organization's ability to satisfy this cell in the knowledge chain better than its competitors will determine its success or failure. Ultimately,

- How quickly can your organization respond to threats and opportunities that arise within the organization?
- How quickly can your organization respond to threats and opportunities that arise from outside the organization?

success is measured by the ability to respond to turbulence outside of the organization by making decisions without having to coordinate and consider all of the factors in a complex business and market environment. Therefore, smart managers set strategies in terms of broad goals and guidelines, and rely on the organizational ability to 'turn on a dime' when the crosshairs of the organizational environment come into focus with the requirements of the market. This is the essence of competitive advantage – a level of responsiveness to environmental conditions that is significantly faster than that of competitors.

And while this may happen sporadically through serendipity, the smart manager makes it happen by preparing the organization to strike when it senses opportunity.

External awareness

External awareness represents the organization's ability to understand how the market perceives the value associated with its products and services. It is also cognizance of market trends, competitive actions, government regulations, and any other relevant market forces that exist outside the organization itself. When coupled with internal awareness, external awareness may lead to entirely new markets.

This is one of the cornerstones of the internet where new business models are sprouting up at an unprecedented pace. The velocity of the internet provides an incredible opportunity to act upon the market's reaction to new products. However, new models for capturing market responses are just as critical. For example, Amazon.com's ability to capture buying trends of many book buyers and then use these to suggest books with similar themes and authors is the very essence of external awareness.

A smart manager recognizes external awareness as more than just a function of extensive focus groups and market research. The smart manager knows that these can often provide false clues. They provide testimony to what the market needs today, or yesterday, rather than what it will need in the future. In the worst case, it provides only the answers that the market thinks you want to hear. The "classic" example is that of New Coke, which, despite heavy market analysis, proved the ultimate folly of most focus groups. The reality is that as markets move at an ever faster pace, market research is reaching the end of its useful life cycle. You simply cannot research a market that has not yet experienced a product or service. In large part that is supporting the astronomical valuations that many internet companies are realizing. These companies have proven the best indication of a market's acceptance is not market research but actually putting a product in front of a market and seeing how it responds. This accelerates the knowledge chain and leads to a much higher level of confidence on the part of investors and consumers.

The cells of organizations that are not knowledge driven look like this:

	Internal	External
Awareness	Poor internal awareness is indicated by extensive use of organization charts, management by edict, lack of knowledge sharing, and static policies and procedures.	Protracted customer feedback loops result from belabored market research and a reliance on product branding.
Responsiveness	New ideas are stifled by corporate memory, a hierarchical command and control structure, and extensive departmental organization.	Slow distribution channels result in standardized products, long durations between innovation cycles, and extensive emphasis on internal rate of return.

In organizations that are knowledge-driven, all four cells are permeable, allowing the immediate transfer of knowledge between the cells.

The economics of knowledge

Return on time

More than 130 years ago, Karl Marx revolutionized political and economic thought with the publication of his manifesto *Das Kapital*. In it, he called for a world economy in which the workers owned the factors of

The cells of organizations that leverage knowledge look like this:

	Internal	External
Awareness	Always collectively aware of its strengths and weaknesses across structural silos and functional boundaries.	Constantly removing filters between the market and its innovative capacity to form true partnerships with prospects and customers.
Responsiveness	Able instantly to organize skills based on an unfiltered assessment of the internal awareness of its resources and external market demands/opportunities.	The final measure of instinct is a perpetual ability to meet the market on its own terms – even when the market cannot articulate these and a clear return is not present.

But, the smart manager recognizes that proficiency in any one of these four quadrants is not enough. Success is measured by the speed with which knowledge flows through these four links. This is return on time.

production. Today, his vision of a grand communist society lies in tatters. It is supremely ironic, then, that at the end of the twentieth century, the most competitive bastions of capitalism have surrendered ownership of their most valuable factor of production knowledge to the workers.

Every company should work hard to obsolete its own product line ... before its competitors do.

Philip Kotler, *Marketing Management*

This was not entirely intentional. It just so happens that knowledge has become the most important factor of production for the information economy, and knowledge resides in the minds of the workers. This is a dramatic change in thinking for most economic models, and requires a fundamental reappraisal of the way organizations manage this newly empowered resource.

Simply put, the value proposition for the modern enterprise needs to be reassessed. A smart manager knows that the paradigms and yardsticks of the past few hundred years can't be used to value the organization of the 21st century. Whatever knowledge is, wherever it resides, however it is managed, few of us would argue that it is not an essential part of our individual and organizational ability to innovate, compete and succeed.

Whether or not economists adapt their theories to make allowances for these new phenomena, many companies are already mapping their futures in the expectation of an infocratic economy – ruled by the best-informed and most-innovative players. Knowledge management is a crucial component of their strategies.

Traditional economic theory contends that the benefit to a company derived from each additional item it produces diminishes over time, since the company is unable to make each additional item as efficiently as it could the initial items, due to a scarcity of high-quality input resources. This law of diminishing returns predicts that the great industrial giants of the west would inevitably stop growing as they exhausted the most efficient factors of production. But, rather than shrink, these countries have continued to grow at an even faster pace.

Economists of old neglected to consider one factor of production that flies in the face of prevailing economic theory – ideas. While traditional physical objects are indeed subject to scarcity and diminishing returns, the number of possible ways in which those physical objects can be rearranged to create something of greater value is so vast, the prospects for economic growth are far greater than economists would normally have us believe.

The smart manager knows the "magic ingredient" is innovation. Rather than encountering diminishing returns, those companies with the best new ideas can expect increasing returns, as the costs of their products are invested in product design knowledge, which is amortized over the number of products sold. In addition, the more successful a knowledge-oriented company is, the more it is able to generate new knowledge, which begets even better products.

KILLER QUESTIONS

How important is innovation to the success of your company? How well is innovation positioned in your corporate mission statement?

Intellectual capital: a new measure of knowledge

As companies become increasingly dependent on their internal knowledge for their success and growth, their value is shifting from physical assets to the intangible assets of knowledge.

Several organizations have attempted to attach a value to their knowledge assets, based on the belief that a clearer measure of this resource will make it easier to manage. Measuring this "intellectual capital" is, however, no easy task. Intellectual capital can include such diverse and loosely defined resources as employees' knowledge and skills, customer relationships, employee motivation and knowledge-supporting infrastructures.

Nevertheless, some well-known examples such as Swedish insurer Skandia AFS have made significant inroads into this field. They believe it is "better to be roughly right than precisely wrong," and see their efforts as a first step in understanding this ethereal resource more closely. They even go so far as to publish details of their intellectual capital as a supplement to their Annual Report.

Much talk has surrounded this new form of capital which is commonly divided into three categories:

- *intellectual capital*

- *customer capital*

- *structural capital.*

Simply put, intellectual capital represents the sum total of what your employees know. Its value is at least equal to the cost of recreating this knowledge.

Customer capital represents the value of the bond between you and your customers. This is not just a matter of brand loyalty. *Customer capital* considers how well you are able to understand your customers, their changing needs and requirements. Its value is at least equal to the cost of creating a new customer.

Structural capital represents the reduction of intellectual capital and customer capital to product or service. The faster you can do this, the greater your structural value since it does not go stale and become susceptible to competitors.

The total of these three forms of capital is often considered to be the difference in value from book value to market value. However, even this is short-sighted since market value may suffer in the short term while intellectual capital is converted to structural capital and new innovations are being built.

KILLER QUESTIONS

What percentage of total profits come from products and services introduced within the last year?

Perhaps the easiest way to understand the value of these forms of capital in any organization is to look at how they are measured within the knowledge chain as return on time.

$$ROT = (\% \ of \ Profit/100) * (\ Sustained \ Years \ / \ \#Years \ )$$

This equation assesses how innovative an organization is by measuring its ability to sustain innovation over a period. The higher the ROT, the more innovative and competitive the organization.

Smart quotes

What prevents companies from creating the future is an installed base of thinking – the unquestioned conventions, the myopic view of opportunities and threats, and the unchallenged precedents that comprise the existing managerial frame.

Gary Hamel, *Competing for the Future*

Edvinsson co-authored *Intellectual Capital: Realizing Your Company's True Value by Finding Its Hidden Brainpower*. As a vice president and Director of Intellectual Capital at Skandia AFS, he has put knowledge management, aka intellectual capital on the map – or the books so to speak. He was one of the first executives to identify a means for reporting on the intellectual capital of an organization as part of its yearly financial report.

For example, a company that for the past five years has derived 50% of its profit for each year from products that have been introduced in that same year, has an ROT of 2.5. Not bad. However, a company that for ten years has derived 100% of its yearly profit from product introduced in the last three years would have an ROT of 3.3. Even better.

A smart manager will note that this sort of simple analysis masks the complexity of multiple product lines and varying profit contributions by each line. In fact, a complete ROT analysis must look at the lifecycle and contribution of every product over the time period being measured.

ROT	% profit	Number of years	Sustained years
2.5	50	1	5
3.3	100	3	10
2.3	70	3	10
1.0	100	20	20

However, even a simple analysis of available public data provides a clear sense for where your organization stands in its industry relative to its competitors. For example, consider that if you are in the high technology market for integrated circuitry, at least 80% of your profit must come from products introduced in the last 24 months. If not, you are out of business.

The last thing to keep in mind about ROT is that it's a relative measure. There is no absolute measure. As with any other measure of return (return on investment, internal rate of return, return on assets, etc.) you need only do better than your competitors in your market's context to be successful.

2

Cornerstones of Knowledge

At this point in the book we can accept that there are compelling business cases for the "why" of knowledge management. But this still does not answer the "what." There is no denying the rapid and overwhelming hype which has greeted the field of knowledge management.

But, although there is much heat in the knowledge management field, there is very little light. Widespread lack of understanding exists about how to implement knowledge management effectively, or even what it is. Indeed, one has merely to try to find a widely accepted definition for knowledge management to realize the extent of confusion that exists.

Here are two definitions:

- "Knowledge management ... embodies organizational processes that seek synergistic combination of data and information processing capacity of information technologies, and the creative and innovative capacity of human beings."[1]

- "Finding out how and why information users think; what they know about the things they know, the knowledge and attitudes they possess, and the decisions they make when interacting with others."

Is there any reason why users shouldn't be confused with definitions such as these? The smart manager knows that if there is anything at all to knowledge management, it should be capable of a succinct definition. Indeed, this is the case. Put succinctly:

Knowledge management is the leveraging of collective wisdom to increase responsiveness and innovation.

It is important that you discern from this definition three critical points. This definition implies that three criteria must be met before information can be considered knowledge:

- Knowledge is connected. It exists in a collection (collective wisdom) of multiple experiences and perspectives.

- Knowledge management is a catalyst. It is an action: leveraging. Knowledge is always relevant to environmental conditions, and stimulates action in response to these conditions. Information which does not precipitate action of some kind is not knowledge. In the words of Peter Drucker, "Knowledge for the most part exists only in application."

- Knowledge is applicable in unencountered environments. Information becomes knowledge when it is used to address novel situations for which no direct precedent exists. Information which is merely "plugged into" a previously encountered model is not knowledge.

These statements introduce another distinction that the smart manager keeps clear. There is most certainly a difference between knowledge and its management, and information and its management. Too many organizations have gone off creating what they thought was a knowledge management application, only to be disappointed by the results. Their results were actually reasonable and admirable, but most misguided. If you are going to invest in knowledge management, you must be sure to understand how it differs from information management.

- Information management consists of preplanned responses to anticipated stimuli.

- Knowledge management consists of unplanned (innovative) responses to surprise stimuli.

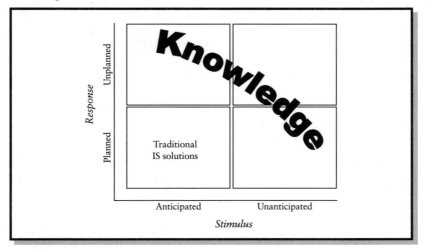

The implication of our stimulus/response matrix is that, to exist, knowledge must be internalized; it must co-exist with intelligence, where decisions are made. For this reason, the primary repository for knowledge is people's heads (at least until we agree that machines have intelligence[2]). Electronic and paper-based "knowledge repositories", then, are merely intermediate storage points for information en route between people's heads.

But before we become too zealous and draw too broad a line of distinction between knowledge and information, consider this. It is perhaps axiomatic that a knowledge-driven enterprise is often only as effective as the information from which it learns. Information and information systems in a knowledge-driven enterprise must be accurate, timely, available to those who need it, and in a format that facilitates use. In most learning organizations, the tests of information and information systems are simple:

- How does this information add value to the decision process?

- How can it get to the people who need it?[3]

A *taxonomy for knowledge management*

But there is obviously more needed to develop a complete understanding of knowledge and its management than these simple ideas. Indeed, the smart manager recognizes that there are different types of knowledge, each with its own specialized characteristics and needs. The best way to build this understanding is to divide knowledge management into two categories:

- *The complexity of the knowledge* – This refers to the degree to which the knowledge can be easily understood and communicated to others. All knowledge exists on a continuum between tacit knowledge and explicit knowledge.

- *The functions or applications performed to manage the knowledge* – Knowledge-management solutions can be reduced to combinations of four functions, characterized by the type of connection each maintains. These functions or applications are known as Intermediation, Externalization, Internalization, and Cognition.

SMART PEOPLE TO HAVE ON YOUR SIDE:

MICHAEL POLANYI (1891–1976)

A modern-day renaissance man, Polanyi was everything from scientist to philosopher. As a Hungarian medical scientist his research was mainly done in physical chemistry. He turned to philosophy at the age of 55. His works, including *Personal Knowledge*, were among the first treatises on how knowledge is created and used. First to identify the difference between tacit and explicit knowledge, Polanyi's theory is about how human beings acquire and use knowledge. It is action-oriented and about the process of knowing. He was adamant about the intrinsic value of tacit knowledge and believed it to be the source of all explicit knowledge. Knowledge does not exist without the human intervention, and herein was the genesis of knowledge being much more than information. Knowledge is internalized and personal. His theories are the foundation to many newly created ones which seek to explain some of the paradoxes of today's stock market.

The complexity of knowledge: tacit vs explicit knowledge

All knowledge can be classified according to its complexity on a continuum from explicit to tacit. Michael Polanyi identified the distinction between these two types of knowledge in 1966.[4]

Explicit knowledge is knowledge that can be articulated in formal language and easily transmitted amongst individuals. Tacit knowledge, on the other hand, can be described as personal knowledge embedded in individual experience and involving such intangible factors as personal belief, perspective, instinct and values. Simply put, explicit knowledge which can be compressed into a few summary symbols that can be encoded by language (i.e. written word) and/or machine. By its nature, it is capable of being widely distributed or diffused. Knowledge of the more tacit kind cannot be encoded and can only diffuse in face-to-face, synchronous communication models.

Clearly, Polanyi's spectrum challenges our earlier premise that knowledge must be internalized. But his views were formed before the information revolution, which effectively raised the bar for what constitutes knowledge in today's enterprise. Polanyi's explicit knowledge is more appropriately referred to as information in the context of our discussion. But it is a widely accepted framework that you should be familiar with and one that we will refer back to for the purpose of illustration.

Explicit knowledge, because of its nature, is typically captured and exchanged throughout the organization. The smart manager recognizes the challenge of explicit knowledge as one of handling the sheer volume of information that is available. On the other hand, while tacit knowledge potentially can represent great value to the organization, it is, by its very

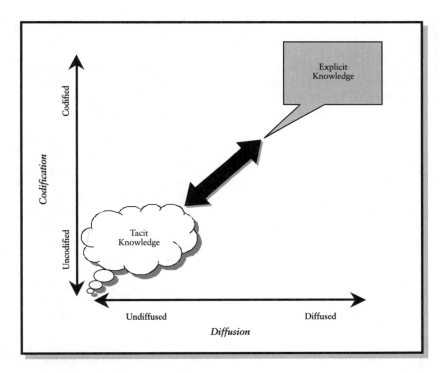

nature, far more difficult (sometimes impossible) to capture and diffuse. The challenges represented by each type of knowledge at a very high level are the same: to build a bridge between seekers and providers of knowledge. But, from a practical level, the challenges are very different. Explicit knowledge can be transferred quite adequately with the help of electronic tools. On the other hand, the most efficient way to convey tacit knowledge throughout the organization is face-to-face. Practices such as apprenticeships, mentoring and communities of practice prove effective.

SMART MANAGERS BUILD KNOWLEDGE COMMUNITIES

Buckman Labs is well known in the knowledge-management circle as a progressive company with regards to knowledge management. Its CEO, Bob Buckman is a smart manager, who sees value in rewarding and incenitivizing staff to share what they know and to collaborate on decision-making.

In 1997, management at Buckman Labs teamed with outside resources to specifically develop an enterprise-wide human resource knowledge-sharing system focused on simplifying the identification of competencies within Buckman Labs' personnel, and preserving and sharing the decision-making processes smart managers execute within Buckman. Much of the explicit knowledge stored in the heads of key personnel was formalized in a series of on-line profiles. The knowledgebase constructed from these profiles provides the company with the ability to match its competencies, experiences and skills to changing market demands and customer needs.

As a result, knowledge communities are built in real-time based on explicit linking of talent and experience to situation. Buckman personnel report an increased level of confidence in approaching new business and more aggressive attitude towards facing new situations.

The real proof is in the company's long-term return on its knowledge management investment. Bob Buckman reports that revenues from new product sales (what we referred to as *return on time*) have more than doubled from 15% to 35%.

Consider that an organization's accounts payable process may consist of a series of well-defined steps, and the rationale behind decision-making in each of those steps is clearly laid out and can be explained to others easily.

The knowledge embedded in this process would be primarily explicit knowledge. Another process, such as an Account Manager's activities, may be more tacit. A knowledge of customers, their interests and concerns, and the skills required to fulfill their needs, differences amongst customers and approaches that work with each respectively is based largely on experience developed over time, inherent abilities, and an empathy with the customer. This is the realm of tacit knowledge. The approaches to handle them and communicate them are vastly different. This is why Zen masters are led to impart their wisdom over a number of years to a small band of intimate and trusted disciples, whereas bond traders communicate anonymously on a worldwide basis and in a matter of seconds on the basis of well articulated price/quantity data.

For decades, organizations have focused their information-technology investments on explicit knowledge, rather than tacit knowledge. There are three reasons for this:

- Explicit knowledge is often conveyed as a standard part of most transaction-based information systems.

- It is much easier to convey and capture than tacit knowledge.

- We have an inherent mistrust of anything that cannot be conveyed objectively and quantified.

Witness how financial statements reflect only tangible assets, even though the most valuable resources which a company has (i.e. the thinking ability and knowledge of its employees) is not captured at all, with the exception of rare organizations such as Skandia AFS.

An organization's most valuable knowledge is often tacit. Because explicit knowledge is so easy to convey, competitors can easily acquire similar knowledge. They cannot learn and create tacit knowledge so easily – thus, for the company that is able to leverage tacit knowledge, it has a much more powerful tool for competitiveness at its disposal.

There is no doubt that tacit knowledge plays a more important role in distinguishing companies in terms of success. For this reason, an ability to expand the level of tacit knowledge throughout an organization is regarded as one of the core objectives of knowledge management. It also happens to be one of the most difficult.

The smart manager understands the different challenges faced between explicit knowledge bases and tacit knowledge bases. The primary challenge when facing explicit knowledge is to manage its volume and ensure its relevance.

> **Smart quotes**
>
> Everybody experiences far more than he understands. Yet it is experience, rather than understanding, that influences behavior.
>
> Marshall McLuhan

A common malaise facing organizations is information overload, as the levels of explicit knowledge become so overwhelming that they cannot be appropriately filtered, and applied or connected at the right point and time.

For tacit knowledge, however, the challenge is to formulate the knowledge into communicable form in the first place. Indeed an initial and significant challenge faced by the smart manager embarking into knowledge management is to challenge the inability of traditional information systems to codify tacit knowledge.

But it's not just the information-systems challenge. In many cases, knowledge believed to be tacit, is only so labeled because no-one has ever taken the time or energy to codify the knowledge. Users may be too quick to reply "It's just too difficult to explain, it defies explanation." This is a real problem and one not easily resolved.

The first response is often to look for bodies of uncoded knowledge that can be translated into printed/captured languages and thus made explicit. This may only create further problems as knowledge workers recoil by hoarding even more of what they know. Recognize that not all knowledge can be codified, and not all knowledge workers see codification as a positive step.

Knowledge-based strategies must not focus on collecting and disseminating information, but rather on creating a mechanism for practitioners to reach out to other practitioners. Such mechanisms, like communities of practice, have special characteristics. They emerge of their own accord: three, four, twenty, maybe thirty people find themselves drawn to one another by a force that is both social and professional. They collaborate directly, use one another as sounding boards, and teach one another. They are built on a bond of obvious *trust*: a key word for any knowledge-management solution.

Communities of this sort are difficult to construct and easy to destroy. They are among the most important structures of any organization where thinking matters, but they almost inevitably undermine its formal structures and strictures. Remember that knowledge is connected. For information to be transformed into knowledge you must recognize, support and administer the connections and, most importantly, the people who are the ultimate owners of all knowledge.

Later in the book we will see how this has very tangible results in helping to translate amorphous intellectual capital into structural capital – products and services.

Communities of practice

Informal

- rise up around social connections and common interests

- can be both functional and cross-functional

- most common type – organic, grow on their own.

Formal

- develop as an outgrowth of empowered teams

- tend to be cross-functional because they reflect team composition.

You can leverage informal communities of practice as a model for formal ones, but how do you ensure that the knowledge links are captured and supported? What are the functions that are required of a knowledge management solution to realize such knowledge transfer?

Knowledge-management applications

There are four key applications of knowledge management. These functions are based on a model which regards knowledge management's primary role as the sharing of knowledge throughout the organization in such a way that each individual or group understands the knowledge with sufficient depth and in sufficient context as to apply it effectively in decision-making and innovation.

These four applications of knowledge management are:

- intermediation

- externalization

- internalization

- cognition.

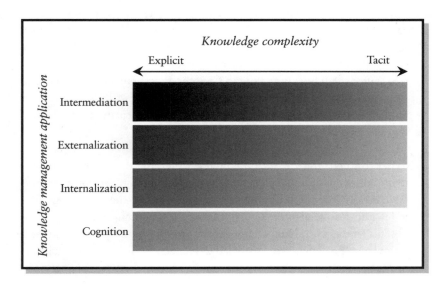

Intermediation

Intermediation is the connection between knowledge and people. Intermediation refers to the brokerage function of bringing together those who seek a certain piece of knowledge with those who are able to provide that piece of knowledge. Its role is to "match" a knowledge seeker with the optimal personal source(s) of knowledge for that seeker. Two types of intermediation are common:

- *Asynchronous intermediation* occurs when externalization and internalization do not occur simultaneously. In this case, an external knowledge repository stores information about the owners of knowledge. Most knowledge bases operate in this way: knowledge is captured and classified in the knowledge base, often before a specific need for that knowledge elsewhere in the organization has arisen. When a knowledge seeker requires that knowledge, the knowledge base can be searched and the relevant knowledge extracted. If explicit knowledge is retrieved, this is internalization. But if tacit knowledge owners are identified, this is asynchronous intermediation. In this case, intermediation is greatly simplified, but, as will be pointed out in Chapter 4, asynchronous intermediation incurs other difficulties. This approach is typically best suited to explicit knowledge, which can be captured more easily in an external storage medium.

- *Synchronous intermediation*, on the other hand, occurs when the externalization and internalization occur simultaneously. Here, knowledge is not stored while being transferred; instead, the knowledge-provider and knowledge-seeker engage in direct communication. In the absence of the central knowledge-repository, the challenge exists to match knowledge-providers with knowledge-seekers. While this approach may appear less efficient than asynchronous intermediation, it is far more common in tacit knowledge transfer, because it permits more sophisticated dialogue between the knowledge exchangers. Communities of practice, the informal groupings of individuals united by a common interest or vocation, and who interact to exchange knowledge with their peers, are an example of the role of intermediation of tacit knowledge.

Externalization

Externalization is the connection of knowledge to knowledge. It refers to the process of capturing knowledge in an external repository, and organizing the knowledge according to some classification framework or ontology. A map or structure of the knowledge collection is provided. The function of externalization is to provide for the sharing of knowledge.

Far too many organizations focus their efforts on how to get knowledge out of their knowledge-management systems, and too little, if any, on getting knowledge into the system. The capture and collection of knowledge occurs in many organizations without regard to formal mechanisms. But a knowledge management system, like an ecosystem, cannot be constantly depleted of its resource without constant replenishment. This knowledge represents the unique advantage of most small companies or companies in incipient markets where staff turnover is low and informal information sharing occurs naturally between a relatively small group of people. However, there are three obstacles to capturing knowledge:

- mobility

- half-life

- threat to specialists

Mobility

Especially in larger organizations and mature or maturing markets, mobility is the daunting challenge of capturing knowledge as employees and their gray matter are constantly moving in and out of the organization.

Half-life

Because knowledge has a limited life-span, people who use it should constantly reevaluate the validity of the knowledge on which they base decisions. The problem, though, is that knowledge is not always overt or easily accessible. Because it's below the surface, it's not examined often. Individuals may assume that a certain process or business method is correct because it has precedent, even if that precedent is based on out-dated premises.

Confusing information with knowledge further exacerbates this phenomenon because we tend to believe that more information creates greater stores of knowledge with which to uniquely differentiate our organizations. In fact, the inverse is true. Greater amounts of information in today's markets tend to level a playing field, since the information is unlikely to be solely available to one organization. Information is simply too easy to replicate and distribute. Knowledge, however, is much harder to replicate outside of an organization's knowledge chain because of the many connections it entails.

Knowledge is not a static source – unlike an information base of contracts, documents, or practices, which can be captured with relative ease. Knowledge is, in large part, found in the sophistication of the methods and attitudes

Smart quotes

The new source of power is not money in the hands of a few but information in the hands of many.

John Naisbitt (Author of *Megatrends*)

by which that knowledge can be consistently renewed. What this means is that knowledge cannot be preserved for very long without losing its inherent value – namely timeliness.

Threat to specialists

Many individuals who have become specialists in their areas of expertise are obviously reluctant to part with their knowledge for fear that it will make their skills less valuable. For the insecure knowledge-worker, knowledge is only limited power. Of course the degree of power still depends on the specifics of the industry. The accounting profession changes little in the course of five years, whereas the knowledge base for engineering and designing integrated circuits changes monthly.

For the organization trying to create a knowledge management system, the challenge is often misstated as simply "knowledge capture" when it is, in fact, "knowledge obsolescence." Having instant access to yesterday's best practices does nothing for a large consultancy like Arthur Andersen if the knowledge is outdated.

Replacing knowledge is much more important – and more difficult – than its simple capture. And doing this stumps most organizations. They realize too late that all their efforts to capture knowledge are nothing more than a casual accumulation of information. Most organizations have been collecting information for some time – but, as we have pointed out repeatedly, that is not knowledge management.

The three components of externalization

Capture and storage of the knowledge in a suitable repository

Knowledge that is stored in someone's brain is not easily accessible to the rest of the organization, so a common repository for all such knowledge is required. This can take the form of a database, a document, a videotape or even a language. It is not necessary that this repository allow for long-term storage of knowledge; in fact, it may disappear as soon as it is retrieved, as in the case of oral communication. The repository for this knowledge should be appropriate for the kind of knowledge being dealt with. For example, numeric data may best be stored in a structured database, while visual knowledge may best be captured using videotape or even in a live performance.

Interpretation of the knowledge to a form that is usable

Many documents in a company may exist only on paper. While they can be scanned, they cannot be immediately manipulated. In such cases, the images can be converted into usable text. Another example is the translation of words from one language to another.

Classification or organization of the knowledge into a format that can be more easily used

This is probably the most difficult of the three functions. It relies on the knowledge possessed by the knowledge-provider to shape the classification of the information into the most usable form. The aim here is to make the knowledge digestible to the knowledge-seeker in the most efficient way possible. For example, an organization which wanted to capture its "best practices" in a database would build a technique for classifying each case or project so that they could be retrieved more easily.

Internalization

Internalization is the connection of knowledge to query. It is the extraction of knowledge from an external repository, and its filtering to provide greater relevance to the knowledge seeker. Closely tied to an externalized knowledge base, internalization reshapes the knowledge base specifically to address the focal point of the query issuer.

There are two distinct aspects of internalization.

- *Extraction of knowledge from the repository, and its deposition into the brain of the knowledge seeker(s)*

  Knowledge should be presented to the user in the form most suitable for its comprehension. Thus, this function may include interpretation and/or reformatting of the presentation of the knowledge. Long lists of figures, for example, are often more easily understood by their presentation in the form of a graph. Another example is the familiar "executive overview" which encapsulates the most vital knowledge at the beginning of a longer document.

- *Filtering the knowledge*

  This means extracting the knowledge relevant to the knowledge-seeker's needs from the mass of information. While users may understand what their need for the knowledge is, they may not fully comprehend the entire field of knowledge in sufficient perspective to be able to extract the relevant knowledge easily. It is thus the function of the knowledge-management solution to assist in the filtering of the knowledge. For example, a team working on a project related to the financial futures industry may request a history of similar projects from a knowledge base, and receive a list of projects which have the greatest degree of overlap with the current one.

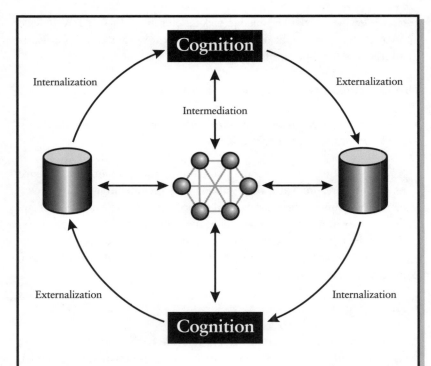

This figure illustrates the relationship between internalization, externalization, intermediation and cognition.

Externalization

Externalization refers to the process of capturing knowledge in an external knowledge repository, and organizing the knowledge according to some classification framework or taxonomy.

Internalization

While externalization captures knowledge, internalization matches the knowledge to a particular user's need to know. Internalization is the extraction of knowledge from the knowledge repository, its filtering to provide greater relevance and, ultimately, a means by which the user can build new bodies of knowledge.

Intermediation

Intermediation links the knowledge seeker with the knowledge and provider of knowledge. While internalization is focused on the transfer of explicit knowledge, intermediation is focused on brokering tacit knowledge. By tracking the experience and interests of individuals, Intermediation can link those that need to know with those who have the knowledge.

Cognition

Cognition provides users with the ability to make quick and spontaneous connections between separate pieces of knowledge by using visual tools for navigation through a complex body of knowledge. The result is the creation of new knowledge – the ultimate goal of knowledge management.

Cognition

Cognition is the linking of knowledge to process. It is the process of making or mapping decisions based on available knowledge. Cognition is the application of knowledge which has been exchanged through the preceding three functions.

In its simplest form, Cognition is achieved by applying experience to determine the most suitable outcome. Chess games are perhaps the most familiar example of simple (although increasingly complex) decision-making. This kind of decision-making is, however, only applicable in contexts where circumstances follow a relatively predictable path. For more complex situations, such as rapidly changing business environments, decision making often takes the form of reliance on limited amounts of information, or even on intuition or feeling. Indeed, such decision-making is usually conducted by humans.

Contrary to popular belief, technology is not a panacea for cognition. Most technology solutions apply to bounded problems, where future predictions are possible based on history. However, the problems and opportunities facing contemporary organizations are increasingly of a "discontinuous" nature, and the predictability of the future is less valid. Thus, machines are unable to do this – only humans are able to generate the "out-of-box" thinking which can address these issues. But cognitive approaches such as visualization may play an important role in helping humans understand the context of a decision.

The fifth application

Though not technically a knowledge-management application, the smart manager recognizes a critical fifth application, measurement. Measurement refers to all knowledge-management activities that measure, map and quantify knowledge and the performance of knowledge-management solutions. This is less a function of knowledge management, than an activity aimed at ensuring that knowledge management is implemented successfully.

Most knowledge-measurement activity today takes two forms:

- *Management accounting efforts to develop financial metrics*

  These metrics are used for performance measurement and incentivization. Few companies have actually commenced activities here, although the ones that have are experiencing some success. (See Chapter 4 for more detail on incentivization.)

- *Activity-analysis efforts*

  This usually involves a more hands-on, yet macroscopic analysis of the statistics describing the activities of knowledge repositories and communication. Such measurement activities are frequently conducted as part of business process analysis and reengineering efforts. Many times, proxies for knowledge activity such as network traffic levels and e-mail distribution lists are used to evaluate the state of knowledge usage.

In either case, a smart manager will orient measurements around the company's vision, and value it according to the contribution they can make. Intellectual capital should be categorized to make it more manageable.

The primary indication of intellectual capital is a proxy measurement, rather than an exact measurement. For example, one department in Skandia uses phone availability as an indication of the efficiency of administrative routines.

Given the uniqueness of each company's measurements, the process of developing and refining the indicators is usually a bottom-up process involving both those who do the measuring and those who are to be measured.

Putting your knowledge to work

Despite the diversity of discussion and opinion surrounding knowledge management, there are essentially three categories of activity currently being undertaken. Smart managers, such as yourself, will, from the outset, determine the approach most suitable to the goals of your organization. This helps to set the expectations for knowledge management, and provide insight into the type of technologies, applications and leadership styles that are necessary. The three categories of activity are:

- the learning organization

- the knowledge library

- mission-critical awareness.

The learning organization
This approach to leveraging knowledge is focused on enabling the organization to handle new business strategies. It is oriented towards cultural reform of organizational attitudes and practices surrounding knowledge. The learning organization focuses on reforming the way people think and learn skills, rather than just on the way they organize their knowledge. The learning organization focuses on team-learning through exchange of the tacit knowledge which each of the members possess. In this way, they are able to develop a "team knowledge", less susceptible to damage through loss of key employees. The objective of the learning organization is to improve levels of innovation throughout the organization.

This approach requires an emphasis on generative learning. Generative learning comes into play when we discover that a problem or gap in our

Nonaka's research focuses on the creation of knowledge process in organizations. Author of several books and papers including: *The Knowledge Creating Company*, NY Oxford Press, 1995; "Toward Middle Up-down Management: Accelerating Information Creation", *Sloan Management Review*, 1998; "The New Product Development Game," *Harvard Business Review*, Jan.–Feb. 1986; "Creating Organizational Order out of Chaos: Self-renewal in Japanese Firms", *California Management Review*, Spring 1998.

In *The Knowledge Creating Company*, he and co-author Hirotaka Takeuchi introduced the world to "organizational knowledge creation," defined as the capability of a company as a whole to create new knowledge, disseminate it throughout the organization, and embody it in products, services, and systems. It is through this process that they believe organizations can continuously, incrementally and spirally innovate and grow.

SMART PEOPLE TO HAVE ON YOUR SIDE:

PROFESSOR IKUJIRO NONAKA, SPECIALIST AND THOUGHT LEADER IN KNOWLEDGE-CREATION

understanding requires new ways of perceiving and thinking. The process of identifying new problems, seeing new possibilities and changing the routes by which we adapt or cope will require rethinking and redesign of our mental models.

Metaskills are the basic tool of generative learning. These help the individual and the organization collectively to manage their skill bases in times of unanticipated events. Metaskills are not typically vocation or technology specific. They enable their carriers to adapt their skills and apply them to new sets of circumstances. In an instinctive company, where knowledge and experience requirements can change almost daily, it's not so much what you know, but what and how quickly you can learn that counts. As a result, the smart manager in the learning organization focuses on and values metaskills as importantly as the base skills in many roles in the organization.

Metaskills are aimed at ensuring three things:

- greater adaptability of individual and group skill sets

- greater aptitude for autonomous decision making

- an emotional aptitude for handling change.

The specifics of the learning organization vary from company to company.

Honda and several other Japanese car manufacturers routinely build "redundancy" into their processes. People are given information that goes beyond their immediate operational requirements. This facilitates sharing in responsibilities, creative solutions from unexpected sources and acts as a self-control mechanism. Swedish business journal Affaersvaerlden uses "piggy-backing" and "team-writing" to speed up learning among new journalists. Interviews and larger articles are routinely assigned as team work, rather than one-man shows. This accelerates the transfer of the seniors' tacit skills and networks to the juniors.

The knowledge library
This approach to knowledge management focuses on enhancing the organization's ability to manage new projects or processes. The smart manager recognizes this approach as one that fits well in situations in which the basic stimuli are not subject to radical and frequent change. Typically, the focus of the initiative is to establish a corporate knowledge base, most typically for the capture and dissemination of best practices and project-related knowledge.

The primary function of the knowledge base is to share insights gleaned from the organization's previous experiences, in the hope that they may find widespread applicability in future projects. Each project, process and case of interest is documented in a loosely structured manner. Supporting documentation is provided where relevant.

In building a knowledge library, the greatest challenge faced by the smart manager is the organization of the knowledge in a way that most closely matches people's needs with the knowledge held by others. Another major challenge is incentivizing people to contribute knowledge to the knowledge base. (See Chapters 3 and 4 for more detail on these issues.)

The knowledge library typically takes a similar form irrespective of the industry or focus of its users. For example, Chevron has created a "best practices" knowledge base, which contains experiences from every assignment including names of team members, client relations, and innovative solutions to problems on site. These are made available to other sites. Numerous strategic consulting firms use a similar approach. In their cases, each team must appoint an "historian" to document the activities of the project.

Often these libraries are built in largely technological solutions, consisting of a flexible document-management/groupware product integrated with a powerful search and retrieval engine, and delivered via a corporate intranet and web browser.

For example, Booz Allen & Hamilton, the international management and technology consulting firm, has linked its 6700 staff members in more than 80 offices around the globe via its intranet-based knowledge management solution, called Knowledge On-Line (KOL). KOL facilitates the exchange of ideas between the company's 6700 worldwide employees. It provides internal staff in 80 offices around the globe with easy and immediate access to the company's current information and best thinking as well as to the company's experts on various topics. The Booz Allen & Hamilton knowledge library is segmented. Strategic applications are concentrated into three key areas:

INTERMEDIATION AT WORK

Management consultants Ernst & Young have a visible and concrete realization of the knowledge broker role. Through their "Ernie" knowledge base, they are able to link the questions of clients to the expertise of consultants.

Ernie, a subscription service, allows clients to enter questions via a web interface. Based on an automated analysis of keywords in the question, the question is routed to a consultant in the organization who has been designated an "expert" in that field. The expert then provides the response to the client, capturing the necessary knowledge shared in the knowledge base. In this way, clients with specific knowledge needs are linked to experts in the knowledge field, irrespective of the geographic location of either of the parties.

It is noteworthy that one of the most valuable features of Ernie is that it acts not as a repository for the knowledge itself, but rather as a repository for contacts. It thus acts more like a "matchmaker" between those who possess certain knowledge, and those who require that knowledge.

- *A knowledge repository*

  This collection represents more than 4000 knowledge content documents cross-filed by topic, industry and geography where the information originates and/or where it is applied. Consultants can make conversational English queries to obtain a list of abstracts entered into the system by the firm's knowledge managers. The documents represent the best and most current of Booz Allen's thinking, ideas and knowledge, making up-to-date information readily available to everyone within the company, a form of internalization.

- *An expert-skills directory*

  This directory provides skills-verification and information on Booz Allen staff members' areas of expertise. The availability of this information enables employees to quickly identify the right people to meet a client's needs, a form of intermediation.

- *Collaboration tools*

  Called KOLaborate, this group of applications allows two levels of collaboration: private communications, as a vehicle for product development and client-engagement teams to work together globally; and public communications, as a virtual knowledge help desk and for discussion groups for promoting new ideas, another form of intermediation.

Mission-critical awareness

The smart manager that needs to leverage knowledge in order to enhance the performance of existing processes will recognize the application as one of mission-critical awareness. These applications must manage large amounts of information and facilitate the intuitive and timely extraction of knowledge from the mass of information (internalization). This approach to knowledge management is also commonly referred to as a knowledge warehouse. Mission-critical awareness applications are often deployed in the field of customer care.

In such an application, a comprehensive overview of the dynamics of the business and the industry in which it competes is provided. The knowledge warehouse contains information about products, distribution channels, customers, competitors, and suppliers. These broad categories might represent segments of the warehouse that provide a different view of the business. The warehouse integrates the collected information into a logical model of different subject areas and makes this information accessible across the enterprise Just-In-Time, when it is required by users to enhance their work.

Notes

1. Malhotra, Y. World Wide Web Virtual Library on Knowledge Management, http://www.brint.com

2. For more on computer intelligence read Ray Kurzweils, *The Age of the Spiritual Machine.*

3. McGill, Michael E; Slocum, Jr., John W. *The Smarter Organization: How to Build a Business That Learns and Adapts to Marketplace Needs.* John Wiley & Sons, Inc., New York. 1994, pp. 14–15.

4. Polanyi, M. *The Tacit Dimension*, Routledge & Kegan Paul, 1966.

3

Knoware: The Technology of Knowledge Management

If the smart manager knows one thing, it is that knowledge management is not just about technology. But, if the smart manager knows two things, the second is that in today's age of technology-driven communication and information-production, the role technology can play to facilitate knowledge management should be examined.

Even though users rank technology only fourth in terms of importance as a component of knowledge management solutions, technology is inescapably a part of all but a small number of knowledge management success stories. However, the components of knowledge management technology are still being defined.

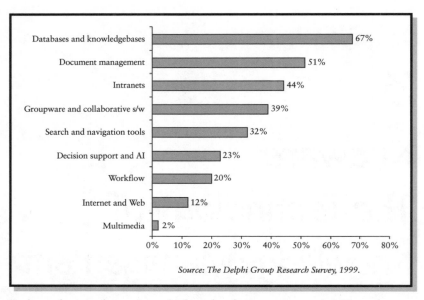

Source: The Delphi Group Research Survey, 1999.

So how do you determine which technologies to invest in? How do you determine which technologies will support the knowledge needs of your organization? The smart manager answers these questions by performing a knowledge audit and mapping the needs of the organization to the knowledge management application framework introduced in the previous chapter.

The chart below illustrates how some commonly used technologies form part of a knowledge management solution. Note that all the technologies are positioned on the explicit side of the diagram, while the solutions listed on the tacit side are all human-based. Technology will not replace the value of and need for face-to-face synchronous communication with regards to tacit knowledge, but you should appreciate that technology can

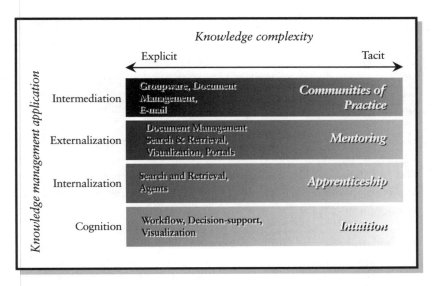

assist in brokering the owners of tacit knowledge and facilitating the creation of people-based networks.

Smart technologies for intermediation

A range of technologies can facilitate intermediation. These technologies are especially valuable for organizations that are highly distributed geographically and therefore less likely to encounter face-to-face or synchronous communication in the normal course of interaction among knowledge workers.

In support of the need for personal communication, Intranets and groupware applications, such as newsgroups and discussion groups, can serve as meeting-places for establishing contact between knowledge-seekers and knowl-edge-providers. They facilitate asynchronous collaboration by multiple in-dividuals and can foster the creation of communities of practice. At a more powerful level, document-management systems, typically used to track the contents and integrity of a document, can be used to track individuals with similar interests within an organization. Electronic yellow pages can also help by creating profiles, or on-line dossiers of individuals (i.e. tracking who they are, what projects they have worked on, what documents they have written, edited, read, etc.). The system becomes familiar with user interests and foci. Subsequently, in response to a user query, these intermediation tools can provide the name, and contact information for probable owners of relevant insight (i.e. tacit knowledge) on the subject of the query.

A wonderful example of intermediation is Sclumberger's use of its e-mail repository as a point of connection between knowledge workers. Sclumberger had developed an e-mail add-on that allows users to nomi-nate e-mail messages for inclusion in a central knowledge base. Since the process was already part of an existing transfer of information the capture was painless. Users could then submit queries that were processed and pointed back to the authors of e-mails with relevant information.

Smart technologies for externalization

Once an organization has mastered intermediation, it must find a means of cataloging the new knowledge that results from connecting people. This can appear to be much easier than it is. Because we have become so accus-tomed to indexing information in the form of documents, databases, and structured forms, we immediately revert to the same techniques for knowl-edge. But the smart manager knows that knowledge is not codified information, and therefore requires a different approach to indexing. Knowledge carries with it the more complex task of making connections between information and people and then, putting information in context.

Consider the complexity of creating and maintaining hypertext-linked world wide web documents, compared with a word-processing file. Links are necessary to form the navigation through a knowledge base, yet they also compound the problem of navigating because they exponentially increase the possible interpretations of any single document. Cataloguing information used to mean searching and finding a set of documents. With knowledge links, any single document can lead to an indeterminate number of other links, making navigation nearly impossible.

Smart quotes

We are drowning in information but starved for knowledge.

John Naisbitt (*Megatrends*)

In addition, the links themselves must change, as must the documents, if the knowledge base is to be kept up-to-date. The links should reflect both the obvious and covert ties between separate forms of information to portray the knowledge value that comes from information in context. Not only is the job of the knowledge user made more difficult, but the maintenance of the knowledge requires significant added resources.

A smart manager will learn to rely on intelligent inventory systems that catalog knowledge both as it is needed, and as it is encountered (i.e. entered). But, in either case, the approach used must be dynamic. Again, recall that we are not categorizing information that can be stored in predefined categories and standard hierarchies, but instead knowledge that is changing continuously. While the former approach is acceptable, it must be coupled with an approach that reassess the relationship of each body of knowledge with every other body of knowledge.

If the knowledge base is vast and virtually unknown by the user community, and/or serendipitous knowledge-discovery is a goal of the application, externalization tools must be a focus of your solution. Seek out document management and search and retrieval tools that do more than just provide a database in which to store documents and other bodies of knowledge. Look to document management and search tools that provide front-ends that provide, either manually or through an automated approach, a means to evaluate the content and source of each document, looking for differences and commonalties amongst the collection.

At the high end, look for portal systems that provide a facilitated means for accessing and utilizing the connections discovered by the externalization tool. These are road maps that depict the landscape of your knowledge base, often in visual terms. Such functionality can uncover connections between concepts found in knowledge collections, connections not previously known or recognized by the knowledge user. With the incorporation of visualization tools, a handful of today's externalization tools can greatly facilitate the navigation of the knowledge base, and the serendipitous discovery of relationships in the knowledge base.

Visualization tools range from the creation of spider-web like diagrams that plot out key concepts uncovered in the automated analysis of document content, portraying the intricate relationships between these concepts; to the creation of virtual solar systems representing the concepts uncovered in your knowledge base, complete with a user starship icon, that permits investigative navigation through the solar system, permitting zooming in and landings for more detail at particular nodes of interest.

Smart technologies for internalization

While externalization may make sense of the knowledge collection, and provide a view into the myriad connections it contains, a smart manager must also provide for each user the ability to impose their perspective into the knowledge base and succinctly pluck out the relevant bodies of knowledge. This, as we discussed in the previous chapter, is the role of internalization. Internalization technology is perhaps the oldest amongst the knowledge-management tools, with its roots in simple search and retrieval engines. But, within the realm of knowledge management, the tools of internalization represent functionality that goes beyond simple word searches, to include functionality such as reformatting of knowledge to more easily convey its value to the user. So, while we continue to deploy search and retrieval tools to provide internalization, within the realm of knowledge management, you should insist upon conceptual retrieval tools. A popular approach is the integration of internalization tools with externalization back-ends, thus providing an individualized view into the externalized knowledge base created.

Smart technologies for cognition

Until now, we have differentiated information from knowledge through the need for linkages and intelligence, or putting the information in context. However, you should know that both the links and the information need to follow certain rules in order to convey knowledge. In other words, providing a document and a link to two more documents is necessary but not sufficient for conveying knowledge. It is also crucial to convey the processes or business rules that govern the use of the knowledge, in order for the information to be transferable to people in the organization. This is the role of cognition tools.

Consider a sales person who accesses a knowledge base to assess the buying habits of a competitor's customer. Numerous documents collected over time reflect prior sales opportunities with the prospect and the history of wins and losses to competition. The history is linked to descriptive information about the prospect's business plans, markets, and strategy. These in turn may be linked to recent market activities that indicate the prospect's success in tapping new opportunities. All of this is important information. Yet, can the sales person readily infer why the prospect might buy from his company, given the current circumstances in the market? With enough time and resource, perhaps.

An alternative would be to bundle certain analytical tools along with the knowledge. For example, a simulation tool could create market profiles based on the current demand for the prospect's products. This tool could create the basis for a business case to buy from the salesperson's company rather than a competitor, perhaps due to an increased ability of the salesperson's company to deliver key support in an area of critical importance to the prospect's current market.

Delivering tools with the knowledge is not far-fetched, especially given the rapid proliferation of the Internet and its ability to deploy small, customized applications as part of a typical information transfer. Transfer of knowledge always means transferring the implicit nature of not only "what" but also "how" work is to be done. The latter is a difficult thing to transfer in knowledge work. It is of course much easier to transfer the knowledge of how to handle a customer service call at AT&T than it is to train a CEO on how to create a customer service-driven organization. That is why most knowledge-management cognition tools today are vertically focused. Decision-support trees, case management and decision-support tools are more easily created when focused on a finite problem, such as call centers, and sales force automation.

Finally, a smart manager should consider leveraging the powers of a workflow or a business-process system as a cognition tool. These are tools that provide a means to automate the logic of business processes and execute that process repetitively. The focus of workflow is to ensure process integrity and decrease process time. Vicariously, however, these workflow tools also create audit trails, or histories of the business processes they automate.

Over time, these audit trails represent a body of knowledge regarding how different stimuli affect the business process (e.g. does the process move more readily when certain customers are involved, certain employees are involved, at certain times of the day etc.). While this information is captured in the audit trail, it remains dormant in most products. By integrating investigative/analysis tools, the smart manager can unleash the knowledge within these audit trails, and possibly create automated decisions (cognition at its highest form), by making the workflow system alter process logic based on trends it recognizes.

A knowledge-management system provides users with the ability to expand their understanding over time, as they discover new information about their organization that they did not think to ask. As one knowledge-management user recently told us, "My organization is just a bunch of answers waiting for the right questions to be asked."

> *Smart quotes*
>
> Our age of anxiety is, in great part, the result of trying to do today's jobs with yesterday's tools.
>
> Marshall McLuhan

In summary, most organizations have more knowledge than employees know about. Yet most individuals cannot be expected to ask questions about subjects of which they have no knowledge.

Having put in place knowledge capture, inventory, and transfer, a company can truly claim to have developed a system for knowledge management and in the process laid a significant cornerstone for creating a knowing organization.

More smart things to look for in knowledge-management technology

It is important to point out that knowledge-management technologies of the future will not merely be combinations of existing technologies. We are starting to see the emergence of a new wave of technological solutions that are designed specifically to support knowledge management. While these tools are enhancements of existing technologies, they differ in several important aspects. The best knowledge-management solutions are ideally:

- *Context-sensitive* – the solution should be able to "understand" the context of the knowledge requirement, and tailor the knowledge accordingly. For example, it should be capable of differentiating between animal reproduction and document reproduction, and respond differently in each case.

- *User-sensitive* – the solution should be able to organize the knowledge in the way most useful to the specific knowledge-seeker. For example, I want it to give me knowledge relevant to my current knowledge level, that is easier for me to understand.

- *Flexible* – the solution should be able to handle knowledge of any form, including different subjects, structures and media. It should be able to handle forms that do not yet exist. For example, if I want to learn about gramophone records, it should supply me with knowledge on the technology as well as purchase trends and audio examples of famous recordings.

- *Heuristic* – the solution should learn about its users and the knowledge it possesses as it is used. Over time, its ability to provide users with tailored knowledge should thus improve.

- *Suggestive* – the solution should be able to deduce what my knowledge needs are, and suggest knowledge associations that I myself am not able to make.

Few technologies are able to provide *all* of these features currently. However, knowledge-management technologies of the future are likely to combine existing technologies with significant enhancements. Technology is likely to play a strong role in the management of explicit knowledge, while its role in managing tacit knowledge will primarily lie in facilitating face-to-face knowledge transfer (i.e. brokering knowledge-providers). Additionally, technology will assume many of the routine work tasks of the past, freeing people to focus on knowledge-intensive activities which require human understanding and insight.

In the future, we are likely to see technology as a useful component of the following roles:

- Technology will be the key solution for the automated capture, organization, dissemination and sharing of explicit knowledge. Sophisticated integrated knowledge bases which provide all levels of knowledge management functionality will become widely used.

- Technology will be an enabler for tacit knowledge where it facilitates human interaction in those cases where such interaction was not previously possible. For example, multimedia Internet meeting software will permit members of a team to interact even if the members of the team are on opposite sides of the world. And, it will identify who within a community (i.e. an enterprise) should be a member of the meeting by nature of their interests and background.

- Technology will begin to reshape the organization by taking over the role of all routine work, as well as circumventing inflexible organizational structure, and permitting the establishment of direct interaction between any parties in the organization who wish to communicate.

- Technology solutions of the future are likely to embrace all four of the knowledge-management functions, intermediation, externalization, internalization and cognition.

Knowledge audits

Before we end this discussion on technology, we should investigate the fifth application of knowledge, measurement. In the last chapter, measurement was introduced, not as a knowledge-application, but as a parallel application relating to each of the four knowledge-applications. Are there tools that automate and/or facilitate the measurement of knowledge and knowledge–management initiatives? The answer, put simply is yes. These tools fall under the general category of knowledge audits.

Knowledge audit tools and methodologies are perhaps the most strategic and fundamental investment a smart manager will make with regards to a knowledge-management initiative, because they will provide the level of insight necessary for setting the right expectations, gauging investment, and increasing the chances for a successful outcome.

Many managers espying the world of knowledge management can quickly become bewildered. Fervor is soon turned to bewilderment. Smart managers recognize from the outset that embarking on knowledge management is far more complicated then a simple system design. They know that it is not a matter of just picking the right technology. Indeed, even approaching the problem with a proven systems design effort proves ineffective.

Knowledge management represents, for most organizations, a completely new and different environment in which they are attempting to bring structure and control to something that is typically without boundaries.

Unlike the automation of a structured and predictable application, such as an Accounts Payable system, knowledge-management forces the designer and developer to delve into processes that almost defy formal procedure or rules. There is little to measure, analyze and use as the foundation for a sound system design. As a result there is little precedent upon which to establish an ROI.

Knowledge management forces you to look at informal networks and protocols, myriad approaches to sharing experiences and know-how, as well as any and all cultural, technological and personal elements which spur creativity and innovation in response to changing stimuli.

In order to manage knowledge, it must first be measured, but how? Knowledge is a moving target.

One way to look at the challenge and opportunity of knowledge management is to revisit the matrix of stimuli and responses that we used to differentiate information management from knowledge management earlier.

To recap – An organization is a series of responses to stimuli. Traditional information systems have provided solutions for planned responses to anticipated stimuli (think of an ERP system/accounting/payroll/order processing/etc.).

From the standpoint of business value it can be effectively argued that the three quadrants labeled *knowledge* in the framework previously presented in Chapter 2 (the unplanned responses to unanticipated stimuli) represent a much greater competitive advantage for organizations than the transaction quadrant. Identifying the forces which enable or prevent an organization from effectively engaging its market in these quadrants is essential in building knowledge management practices and solutions.

In conducting research for their book, *Corporate Instinct*, authors Koulopoulos, Toms and Spinello discovered there is no simple way for conducting such a knowledge audit. The unpredictable and often informal nature of knowledge sharing in an organization defies structured measurement. While one might conceive of doing a series of interpersonal studies, this is not practical for two reasons. First, factors such as the responsiveness of an organization to market and internal demands and awareness of core competencies cannot be objectively measured. Secondly, figures which are calculated from actual results of business activity are biased towards the last performance (i.e. the one observed), rather than an organization's inherent ability. To hold any merit, a wide variety of business practices/experiences across the organization over several months would have to be measured, and thus this type of approach is simply impractical.

An auditing tool and methodology is necessary to assess several aspects of the knowledge characteristics of the organization:

- current levels of knowledge usage and communication

- the current state of corporate knowledge management

- identification and clarification of knowledge management opportunities

- identification and clarification of potential problem areas

- the perceived value in knowledge within the organization.

The methodology should assess the effectiveness of an organization by specifically measuring how well it performs within the Knowledge Chain. (See Chapter 2 for more details on the Knowledge Chain.)

The organizational benchmark

No matter what methodology or tool is used, you should first be sure that it can be customized to fit your organization. Knowledge is a very personal thing, and therefore its measurement should use an approach that addresses the issues in a familiar manner. The methodology should not only measure key elements critical to its analysis of the organization's opportunities for, obstacles regarding, and requirements of knowledge management; it should also account for the idiosyncratic factors and influences of each organization.

Be sure that the methodology has a timely approach for being administered *throughout* the organization. By involving individuals from across the organization's staff, it is possible to garner points of view which are frequently overlooked, but which are critical success factors in the management of knowledge. By involving a multiplicity of users, the ability for any single group's perspective to impose prejudice is removed. Since the analysis of findings assesses major trends in opinion across the organization, it uncovers how, as a whole, the perceptions of users and owners of knowledge (i.e. the organization's personnel) shape reality, since there is frequently a causal relationship between perceptions and reality.

In the end, it may not matter what management may think is the organization's potential for knowledge management. The reality is that which is manifest through the experiences and attitudes of its constituents. Equally important, by ensuring that the approach used is timely (i.e. results should be available within weeks), observations are relevant, and user interest does not wane.

As part of the analysis, it is also important to assess the internal factors that can potentially inhibit or promote knowledge-sharing in the organization. Thus the causal effect between these critical elements and the reality of how the organization is functioning from a knowledge-sharing standpoint can be empirically tested.

Benchmarks should be established within the organization for each of the following elements:

- the role of structure

- technology experience, perceptions, requirements

- the impact of culture

- the nature of process management

- sources of innovation

- models of communication

- team-based strategy

- perception of current knowledge-management practices.

Each of these factors should be measured separately, and in conjunction with the others, offering a unique profile of every organization's effectiveness and opportunity in applying knowledge management (KM – see spider chart below). This profile offers insights as to how your organization ranks relative to others in your industry, or even how different groups within one organization rank against another's use of KM. The resulting benchmarks can be used to justify, measure ROI, and precisely assess the value of KM.

Lastly, the methodology used should uncover organizational anomalies amongst the organization-wide findings, and uncover groups within the organization that exhibit positive and negative variances in each of the factors measured. In this manner, you uncover potential points of strength, weakness or opportunity for knowledge management within your organization. By applying targeted interviewing techniques to these specific ar-

In the chart below, the organization profiled with the dotted line has little in the way of formal KM technology or practices, yet it demonstrates an ideal environment for leveraging KM practices and technologies. The organization profiled with the dark black line has KM technology and practices, yet demonstrates an organizational environment that undermines its KM efforts. Neither organization is ideal. Understanding where and how to overcome the inadequacies of each organization is the purpose of a knowledge audit.

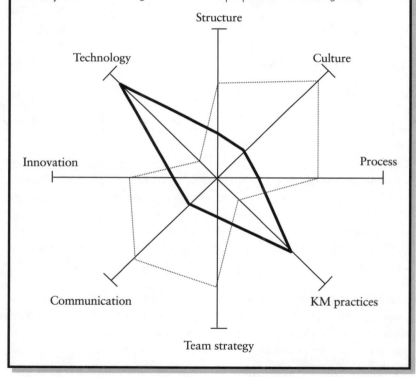

eas of the organization, qualitative assessment can be made regarding the cause of the anomalies. Thus, the organization gains insight into specific formal and informal groups and practices that can either serve as examples of what works within the organization to promote knowledge management, or what should be avoided.

The knowledge audit must be diverse. This is not a technology audit. Again, the smart manager knows that knowledge management is not as simple as selecting the right technology. Thus any measurement tool that is used must assess the relationship between cultural, structural, procedural factors in the organization to technological and infrastructure factors. In this manner, a strategy that includes an intelligent approach to understanding the changes required in culture as well as technology can be derived.

We have witnessed firsthand the incredible results of knowledge audits in our own practice. In one case, the results of an audit affected the turnaround at an R&D department of a major petrochemical company. They had embarked on several knowledge-based initiatives, each of which had full support from upper management. Despite this, the organization's ability to reuse acquired know-how and expertise had not been impacted. The application of the knowledge audit uncovered several obstacles that the efforts to date had ignored. These included cultural differences across various geographic locations, discrepancies in "management speak" versus "management action," and process realities that flew in the face of knowledge-sharing practices. The audit also uncovered an underlying cultural approach to team building, which had been virtually untapped by initiatives. Once these strengths and weaknesses had been identified, an action plan was developed specifically to handle and exploit them respectively.

As a result, minor modifications to existing systems brought about major changes and a real ROI.

At a major federal government organization, the application of an audit uncovered informal approaches to knowledge sharing that could be leveraged in building an automated approach to knowledge management. As a result, the approach taken to technology product-selection, process definitions and design of a taxonomy for the envisioned knowledge base took a dramatic turn from original plans, resulting in a much shortened implementation.

In yet another instance, the audit revealed that, despite high achievement in internal and external awareness levels in this manufacturing company, bodies of knowledge were treated as isolated silos. Thus, despite the levels of knowledge acquired, the overall organization reacted lethargically to changes in stimuli, and required extensive corporate review and approval. Exceptions existed in the form of informal teams that arose almost organically within the organization. By uncovering the obstacles as well as the strengths, minor modifications in technology directions and communication protocols were set in place that enabled this organization to achieve radically positive results.

Ultimately the knowledge audit uncovers the propensity of an organization for knowledge management, the current levels of knowledge management in practice, and the internal factors that either prohibit or promote the further growth and leveraging of both. Without this assessment, attempting to design a knowledge-management system for an organization is virtually futile. Existing opportunities can go unnoticed and thus underutilized, and real obstacles can go undetected.

In the final analysis the knowledge audit may be the smartest thing you do to leverage your organization's knowledge.

Portals

Creating a corporate knowledge portal

Portals are a very specific type of knowledge-management tool. Portals have garnered more attention than virtually any other Internet technology over the past year. *Why?* In no small part, the answer to that question lies in Wall Street's mania with Yahoo!, Lycos, Infoseek, and Excite. Some have gone so far as to call portals the next generation of desktop computing; claiming that what railroads of the 18th century did to build an infrastructure for the industrial revolution, portals will do for global knowledge-work.

What does this have to do with knowledge management? The smart manager recognizes the value of portal technology, not just on the Internet, but behind the firewall. Furthermore, the smart manager is readily able to embrace portals and exploit them internally, because they recognize the premise of portals is not new. Portals have been lurking below the surface of desktop computing for the better part of the past two decades. It's only with the recent proliferation of the Internet that the word "portal" has become the mantra *du jour*. Virtually everyone now using Internet technologies inside or outside the firewall integrates portal visits into their online experience, making the metaphor one of the most powerful since the advent of a windowed desktop.

Why the mad rush? Some reasons are simple and obvious. The rise of internet technology has resulted in a uniquely frustrating experience for nearly everyone using the web. From home users to knowledge workers, it is rare that interaction with a computer involves a single information resource. The simplest search of the web, the most basic knowledge-work involves the coordination of myriad sources of data, processes, and people – not to mention the integration of a multitude of desktop, enterprise, and web-based technologies. Remember, knowledge is not simply the use of information, but the processing of information in context, recognizing the links or connections between one source of information and another. Corporate portals reflect a fundamental transformation in our view of enterprise information management from a series of isolated tasks to the coordinated integration of knowledge.

SMART VOICES

SMART MANAGER USES PORTAL TO SHARE KNOWLEDGE AND EMPOWER CUSTOMER SUPPORT

Customers and account managers alike, of a major US financial advisory group with which we had the opportunity to work, complained of a poorly responding customer-support organization. While the manager of this organization understood that part of the problem lay in delayed and inefficient communication models in the organization, the manager was also smart enough to realize that the solution had to go far beyond the problem.

A myopic view on the role of customer support versus sales, and the organization's overall approach to departmentalized thinking was the part of the problem that only a smart manager would recognize.

There was an underlying culture and belief amongst less enlightened management that customer support and sales were separate and distinct entities, with little value in allowing these bodies to function as a single group. Once the situation was addressed not so much from a "get the customer orders in the hands of the customer-support representatives more quickly" perspective (i.e. put out the fire), but from a strategic view towards what is the best way to actually serve the customer, problem resolutions became nearly self-evident.

Creation of a customer-support portal allowed representatives to get complete perspectives on any customer, including: products currently purchased and the options activated on each; current value of each financial package owned by the customer; and a complete payment history of the customer, including last payments made and date of next payment.

More importantly, the portal made available a customer profile which showed everything the organization knew about the customer including: past experiences with the customer, marital status and number of dependents, and the purchase of products from affiliates of the company (e.g. auto insurance, student loans, mortgages and life insurance). Finally, the system automatically linked new programs, program changes and new products that appeared to be relevant to the customer's profile. This knowledge-base allows the customer-support representative to not only satisfy the initial reason for the customer's call, but to turn inbound calls into outbound opportunities to discuss other issues with the customer. This created a tighter relationship with the customer, a smarter group of customer-support representatives and upselling the customer to products they may never have thought to ask for.

The role of corporate portals is not simply to help individuals make sense of the volume of information at hand, but more importantly to help cope with breakdown in our ability to maintain the underlying connections between these information sources – the basis of knowledge. Take as an example the situation at Boeing where the intranet hosts over 1600 separate web sites in use by 160,000 users.

This incredible influx of readily accessible, yet completely disconnected, sources and streams of information has made it clear that the means for navigating, organizing, and linking information with underlying business processes is woefully inadequate in most organizations. It is in this "middle office" space that corporate portals promise to have the greatest impact.

Welcome to the middle office

As a smart manager, you should recognize that the ideal fit for corporate portals is at the intersection of the front and back office, where negotiation, product differentiation, and competitive advantage thrive. While back-office functions focus on cost management, and front-office functions focus on revenue enhancement, it is in the middle office that profit is maximized and risk is minimized by the ability to coordinate the many information streams, people, and knowledge that create sound business. Simply put, it is where organizations ultimately fail or succeed.

The audience for corporate portals is best defined by the role and function of knowledge workers in this middle office space. While front- and back-office functions have reached a stage of relative equilibrium and parity across most industries (thanks to extensive ERP applications deployment for structured transactions), middle-office workers live in a dynamic and unpredictable world. Any application of technology here has a payback that is measured in orders of magnitude.

You should use portal technology to create a "single point of access," which integrates the highly unstructured nature of knowledge work with the wide variety of ERP, document, and CRM systems already in use within one interface – an interface that will ultimately make pale (i.e. obsolete) the contemporary window-based metaphors you use today.

Today's application-based desktops separate and segregate functions that are intuitively part of the same process. This is like using a different type of phone for every state you want to call. Computer users have suffered this absurdity in quiet indignation, long enough. In this sense it is no less likely that corporate users will turn on their desktop machine to be greeted by a corporate portal than internet users will be to start up in my Yahoo!

Given the impact portals will have on desktop computing you should consider the impact they will have on today's desktop-platform providers. Portals create a new playing field that transcends discussions about operating systems, browsers and applications. A portal is the seamless integration of all three. So although you may be right in thinking of Microsoft Office as a desktop environment (which just happens to be deployed on 50 million desktops), it is not a portal – yet.

Microsoft's intent is to move applications, such as Office, clearly into the portal space by providing a platform of easily integrated application objects. The irony here is that the industry's most visible desktop player may soon be barely recognizable at the desktop.

Although your portal may be using a multitude of Microsoft product components, portals will integrate functions such as word-processing, spreadsheets, database, e-mail, and others into a single unified presentation.

So what does that mean to Microsoft? According to Microsoft, it's not unlike the difference between a TV set and a TV studio. The set is merely a delivery vehicle. TV users could care less about the tools used in a TV studio (read: Microsoft's tools for deploying portal content apps). Microsoft also believes that portals will only increase the demand for desktop applications by making integrated enterprise applications available to a much larger audience.

How close is all of this? Although talked about for some time, practical applications seem to be in close view. The number of products and applications covered by the market for portals is diverse. Adding to the confusion is the fact that the concept of a portal can be used to describe almost any sort of desktop with network access. The smart manager can simplify this by thinking of portals as consisting of two basic components, diversity of content and community. Using these dimensions, a simple matrix can be constructed that classifies any portal application into four categories:

- *Published portals* are intended for large and diverse communities with diverse interests. These portals tend to follow a fairly traditional broadcasting metaphor which involves relatively little customization of content except for on-line search and some interactive capabilities, which would be typical for the web.

- *Commercial portals* offer narrow content for diverse communities. These are the most popular portals today for on-line communities. Although they offer customization of the users interface they are still intended for broad audiences and offer fairly simple content (a stock ticker, news on a few reselected items). Commercial portals are often referred to as "channels" since they tend to aggregate web information into a single visual presentation.

- *Personal portals* are target-specific filtered information for individuals. Some of these portals, such as Individual Inc.'s fax broadcast, actually predate the web. As with commercial portals they offer relatively narrow content but are typically much more personalized with an effective audience of one.

- *Corporate portals* coordinate rich content within a relatively narrow community. These are portals most often built of large-enterprise intranet applications. Since they support decision core to particular mission, the term most often used in describing them is *corcasting*. Their portal content is much broader than that of a commercial portal since there is far greater complexity to the diversity of information used to make decisions in an organization, as contrasted with the individual deciding to buy or sell stock while reading a press release, a news story, and watching the stocks trading volume. A good example would be to contrast a commercial portal such as Excite, with Bank of America's use of Microsoft's Digital Dashboard Portal. Although the metaphors are similar, the latter is clearly a corporate portal.

The dilemma of organization

A fundamental challenge in building a knowledge base is in building a repository that can be used by everyone in the organization. This of course creates a problem – what we call the *dilemma of organization*.

The dilemma of organization recognizes that the party best equipped to organize or classify the knowledge is the knowledge-provider (who has a clearer perspective and understanding of the knowledge, and can thus separate the wheat from the chaff). However, the knowledge-provider frequently does not understand the precise knowledge requirements of the knowledge-seeker, nor the specific context in which the knowledge-seeker plans to apply the knowledge. The knowledge-provider may also not know who the knowledge-seeker is.

Conversely, the knowledge-seeker understands the context in which the knowledge is to be applied, but neither understands the knowledge in sufficient depth nor necessarily knows that it exists, in order to search for it.

To put it simply, the knowledge-provider knows the answer, but not the question, and must thus organize the knowledge by attempting to second-guess the knowledge-seeker's question.

The knowledge-seeker, on the other hand, understands the question, but has insufficient perspective of the answer to know where it may be best found. This translates itself into "information overload but knowledge underload". Poorly constructed knowledge-bases containing huge amounts of information are unable to meet the specific requests for knowledge posed to them.

Designers of Knowledge Management solutions can relieve this dilemma in three ways:

- *Replace asynchronous knowledge transfer with synchronous knowledge transfer*

    Dialogue between knowledge provider and knowledge seeker at the time of knowledge transfer greatly improves the accuracy and relevance of the knowledge transfer, as both parties are able to adjust the other's understanding of their perspective.

- *Incorporate feedback mechanisms into the solution*

    The solution should be able to "learn" from the associations and preferences expressed by the knowledge-provider and knowledge-seeker, and use this information to provide more "accurate" responses to future queries.

- *Make use of tools that combine the speed and efficiency of technology with the "fuzzy" understanding of humans*

    In this way, larger volumes of knowledge can be managed, but greater comprehension of the knowledge being handled improves the accuracy of knowledge categorization and searching.

> *Smart quotes*
>
> At the same time that technology is creating interrelationships, it is also reducing costs of exploiting them.
>
> Michael E. Porter

Externalization tools have been designed to specifically address this need. Through the use of the right tool, providers of knowledge will not have to anticipate the value or context of the knowledge, but rather allow the system to determine the relationship of this knowledge resource to other bodies of captured knowledge. Additionally, internalization tools, if properly used, will augment the knowledge base building functionality of externalization, by allowing the knowledge seeker to impose his/her perspective on the knowledge-base and dynamically, in an intelligent manner, identify that which is relevant to the seeker, from that which is not.

	Knowledge provider	*Knowledge seeker*
The dilemma of organization	Well-equipped to organize (classify) the knowledge, but does not know the context in which it is to be used	Knows the context of the required knowledge, but does not understand the knowledge in enough depth to organize it

What do you know? A road map to internalization needs

A smart manager begins his/her investigation of technology by assessing the reality of and needs of the organization. In the case of internalization needs, think in terms of what your organization knows and what it does not know. A simple grid (below) can help organize your thoughts and priorities. This grid is built on two axes, information sources and the user. Its intersections pinpoint the four possible environments that emerge when these two axes meet. In other words, there is the information you know you know, the information you know you do not know, the information you do not know you know, and the information you do not know you do not know.

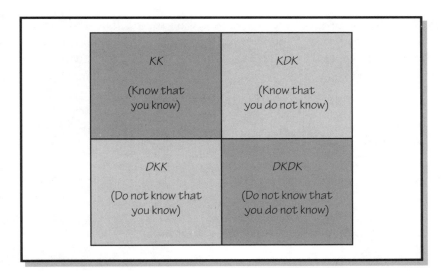

The idea of this grid is to illustrate the different search environments or needs for knowledge access that exist. Each of these in turn dictates a different type of product or search features.

In the situation where the user knows what he/she knows (the top left quadrant), the need is typically for a simple search engine. This is a situation where the volume or geographical distribution of information sources inhibits rapid retrieval. However, the user is aware of the contents and what they need to find, so the research model is simple.

In the case where the user is aware of the inability to access information (the upper right quadrant), the need, at least initially is to gain access to the source.

When the user is given access to information sources, but is unfamiliar with them, and needs to do knowledge discovery, (the bottom left quadrant), there is a need for specialized search and retrieval tools, which augment the user's often naïve preliminary search, and expands it intelligently.

This situation is further complicated in the case where the user is unaware of what it is he/she does not know. Here the combination of a discovery search-tool with a discoverer (e.g. a web crawler) is required.

Killer apps

Is there a killer app for knowledge management?

Is there a compelling business area or process that is more suited than others for knowledge management? Based on discussions with smart managers and users of knowledge-management systems, popular trends with regards to applications do arise.

Straightforward areas such as electronic yellow pages, call center learning and market research were reflected as prime candidates for substantial knowledge-management payback. They are also applications that have natural fit and appeal to the end users – in other words, there is not a lot of arm-twisting necessary to get user buy in. These applications focus on specific business needs that cut across large horizontal segments of an enterprise. Yet, they are still fairly confined in terms of their scope and complexity. The point that should be stressed is the practicality of the applications that have made it the furthest.

4

The Softer Side of Knowledge Management

So you are a smart manager. You know that cultural challenges in knowledge management are your paramount concern. But where do you go from here? How do you address these? In Chapter 3 we introduced the concept of the knowledge audit. A primary outcome of the audit is the identification of what the challenges within your organization are. But, while the specifics of each organization's challenges are unique, the smart manager will recognize that there are some basic universal challenges that will have to be confronted. As a smart manager you should meet these head on. What are these basic issues? – We are speaking of building a community of knowledge sharers, the ownership of knowledge, and incentivization.

In the ideal knowledge-based world, we would all have access to each other's know-how. We would share what we know freely, and we would compete based on a constant flow of new knowledge.

The ideal knowledge-based world is a far cry from today's culture of knowledge-hoarding. After all, what type of person would willingly give up what they know – their most valuable commodity?

Convincing personnel to share their individual knowledge amongst themselves has, for years, been a promising yet elusive goal for many organizations. Given the tremendous upside potential, however, it is no surprise that the quest to coax an organization's members to share their knowledge is as great as it is. Imagine the bounty of untapped opportunity available to your organization if only one of the following were true:

- your newest hired customer-service representative could answer questions as well as the most tenured representative

- each and every product designer was aware of not only every project currently in progress, but also of everything previously tried and discarded, as well as a comprehensive understanding of what went wrong

- every sales rep in the field at a moment's notice could call upon the collective wisdom of your most seasoned veterans.

It is easy to conceive the potential benefits available from providing these types of resources to your organization. A large organization in which all employees have access to the same knowledge, can make the same quality of decisions, and can respond with equal expedience, would be *unstoppable*.

This represents the culture of many entrepreneurial firms defined by a handful of principles where knowledge is stored cerebrally, shared frequently, and readily accessible. Yet the seemingly inevitable problem is that once a firm grows beyond a small group, the accessibility of knowledge is no better than that of organizations a thousand times larger, or perhaps much worse, as smaller mid-size firms often lack the infrastructure and documentation used by larger firms to help locate knowledge sources. The tight-knit startup, where ideas and information flow free, ultimately proves to be *unscaleable*. Its growth outpaces the ability to maintain the level of personal connectivity required for effective knowledge-sharing, and which enabled the innovation which made the initiative possible to begin with.

Transitioning from unscaleable to unstoppable through the strategic management of knowledge-based resources, is a function of how well you manage the connections between *people*, *processes*, and *technology*. These three elements represent the "holy trinity" of organizational transformation, and are the linchpin of effective knowledge sharing.

One approach to knowledge-sharing, used since the beginning of the industrial revolution, reaching a zenith during the 1960s and 1970s, is the grouping of personnel in common, "open air" work environments. A recent and notable example of this is British Airways (BA) "Waterside" campus in Harmondsworth, England. The intent is not unlike Henry Ford's vision of integrating all the means of production into a single facility. But the environment at Ford was a world apart from that at Waterside, where nearly 3,000 BA personnel enjoy the comforts of a corporate village, complete with running streams, a tree-lined main street, cafés, and ample opportunity for solace and contemplation as well as collaboration.

The difference is not simply a matter of philosophy, but of utility: where the assets of production at Ford were raw materials, parts, and the means to assemble them into automobiles, BA derives value from knowledge-based assets. At Waterside, where the focus is the service side rather than the manufacturing aspect of BA's business, intellectual capital is optimized by creating an environment that is ripe for sharing.

BA has recognized the value of serendipitous innovation derived from ad hoc meetings and the free-flow of ideas. But simply allowing personnel to wander about such a facility may otherwise lead to a mammoth "water cooler" effect, with unmanageable and unproductive hordes of employees drifting about without concern, or access to, the elements of work. The difference at Waterside is a strategically designed infrastructure comprising open work-areas, cordless phones, laptops, and a massive wireless network, which allows BA personnel to "plug-in" (although no physical connection is required) and work virtually anywhere within the facility. This is in contrast to the discontinuous collections of cubicles and meeting rooms that define most large corporate campuses, often organized by hierarchical associations rather than functional workgroups. Waterside allows virtual teams to assemble, collaborate, and disband, without losing the continuity of their efforts.

At Waterside, BA has acknowledged the value of sharing knowledge, facilitated by the synergistic junction of people, processes and technology. The desired result, which will ultimately be measured by the sustained competitiveness of the organization, is greater innovation and responsiveness to market demands.

But has BA achieved all, or even one, of the three objectives mentioned above? Clearly they are closer, but there is a subtle, yet critical element missing from their strategy. At Waterside, the sharing of knowledge is facilitated by bringing individuals together, either physically within the open workspaces throughout the campus, or virtually vis-à-vis communication technologies such as video conferencing, groupware and telephones. Both explicit knowledge (e.g., documents and data) and tacit knowledge (e.g., personal beliefs, perspectives, and values) are exchanged during the collaboration. But what is left after the team disbands? While there may be a record of the explicit knowledge exchanged, it is likely that the real value of the collaboration takes a tacit form, in the epiphanies, experiences, and insights that result. Without the ability to transform this tacit knowledge into a sharable format, its benefit to the rest of the organization is lost, substantially diminishing its value.

Knowledge-sharing strategies must not focus only on collecting and disseminating information within isolated groups, but also on creating a mechanism for practitioners to reach out to and learn from each other – not limited to a finite group in a snapshot of time, but the entire organization over an infinite period. This requires more than just the alignment of people and processes, but the strategic application of knowledge management technology.

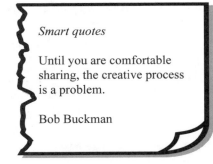

Smart quotes

Until you are comfortable sharing, the creative process is a problem.

Bob Buckman

An architecture for sharing knowledge

There is no dearth of opinion on what comprises knowledge management. What has been lacking, however, is a standard framework that encompasses both the business objectives involved with knowledge-sharing initiatives and technologies available to address them. The model introduced in Chapter 2 and further refined in Chapter 3, that breaks knowledge management into four applications: Intermediation, Externalization, Internalization and Cognition, we believe, is the best approach thus far. It builds on the model of knowledge-sharing offered by Ikujiro Nonaka, illustrated in his seminal book *The Knowledge-Creating Company*.

These functions are based on a model which regards knowledge management's primary role as the sharing of knowledge throughout the organization in such a way that each individual or group understands the knowledge with sufficient depth and in sufficient context as to apply it effectively to decision making and innovation.

Although each of these four areas needs to be considered in creating a knowledge sharing environment, the true crux of knowledge sharing has to do with the process of externalization. As we have already seen, this refers to the process of capturing knowledge. This is where the tacit is transformed to the explicit.

From a technology perspective, this is not simply a matter of organizing information "chunks" into a visual hierarchy based on content, a capability of many document management systems, but rather capturing the contextual relationships. This is the difference between explicit data, where content is known yet context is missing, and "meta data" or the attributes surrounding content which describe its value and relationship to the knowledge base.

More apropos is the commonly misused term "meta knowledge" referring not to the prosaic attributes of format, proximity, and magnitude of the knowledge chunk, but to situational context surrounding its creation and purpose within the organization. For example, when a decision is made and recorded, what should be captured is not only the outcome (easily converted to an explicit form) but also the context of the information which lead to it, the situation of the participants involved, and the contributing factors which alone may not seem related, but when combined with the former, provide the complete story. This may manifest in a new product direction, inspired by the move of a competitor, reinforced by a recent request from the field, and put into action by an ad hoc development team. Without the means for externalization, the historic value is lost – each event is recorded separately (if at all) and any ability to recall the lessons learned during the occasion will be limited to those directly involved. Within a knowledge management solution, however, each piece of the process is identified based on its related context, to be later recalled by querying on any of the linked components.

KILLER QUESTIONS

Do you consider your co-workers to be predominately knowledge-sharers or knowledge-hoarders?

Creating a knowledge-sharing culture

However powerful, the functions of a knowledge management solution are of no use without willing participants. In order for the knowledge base to have value, it must be used by the entire organization. Anything short provides an incomplete picture of the organization's knowledge resources. This is not simply a matter of building an effective system, but creating a knowledge sharing culture within the organization.

Building community

First and foremost a smart manager recognizes the need for community in the organization. If there are no such communities, any attempts to propagate knowledge are futile. While incentivization, discussed in detail later in this chapter, is a requisite to knowledge sharing, you must first realize the importance of creating a group within the organization that can help people to find very self-centered reasons for sharing knowledge.

In one pharmaceutical company I worked with, a very strong community spirit was discovered. It existed on two planes, geographically and project-wise. The project communities were examples of groups with a common cause (i.e. to get a drug to market). This coupled with a general atmosphere of openness throughout the organization created a group dynamic that could be, and was used as a starting point to build knowledge-based communities. The introduction of simple technology changes and process changes, created a system in which employees could easily transfer lessons learned far and wide throughout the organization, not just in their own drug team.

One caveat, however, is that while often important role models, existing communities are not always beneficial to knowledge sharing. In the same pharmaceutical company, communities that were built around geographic location were seen as counterproductive to knowledge sharing. Too great an allegiance was associated with one's physical place of employment. Employees in one location were far less apt to share knowledge with employees in another location. Social events and management directives reinforced through example were necessary to break down the walls between physical plants.

What is most important is to look beyond traditional organizational constructs, such as workgroups and geography, and look for areas of natural coalescence.

Look for the existence of such groups in your organization. If you discover any, leverage them to their full potential for they possess the cultural fertile ground on which knowledge management can thrive. Often these informal groups (communities of practice) have self-constructed within an organization outside of a hierarchy. No one said to these people "go off and become the knowledge-management unit or the coaches or the knowledge intermediaries," but they did it anyway. Why do these communities exist? Out of survival and a sense of common purpose. Each of these can be fundamental approaches to building formally these communities.

Survival is a very powerful instinct. Put a body of people in jeopardy and they will band together in order to protect themselves. Communities of practice began at AT&T after two major divestitures. At GM they sprang from the threat of bankruptcy. Business not as usual made people realize they had to cooperate in order to survive. But, this crisis oriented reengineering of practices is not necessary. But, what we can learn from it is that given a real common focus or sense of purpose, individuals are far more likely to band together and cooperate. To share what they know in order to reach a common cause. Communities of practice started in the big consulting firms (e.g., KPMG, Booz Allen, Bain and Company), not out of survival but out of a common drive to increase profits and leverage internal assets. While most other types of organizations were focusing their efforts on streamlining production cycles and increasing product profitability, these consultancies – with no real product other than intellect, looked inward and realized that by sharing what they

Smart quotes

I use not only the brains I have, but all that I can borrow.

Woodrow Wilson

knew, they could leverage their collective experience and provide not only a better product, but one in far less time.

Other examples of community exist in society. Families are a perfect example. One need only observe a family preparing for diner, setting out on a vacation or preparing to start the typical day, to witness the power of community. Almost instinctively individuals rely on one another for certain needs and tasks. Constant communication occurs to keep the rest of the community aware of progress, encountered hurdles and known work arounds. Medical teams performing a serious procedure on a patient, or a team of flight attendants, pilots and co-pilots in mid air, exhibit similar behavior. These groups function as one virtual unit, openly communicating what they observe and know, reacting to each others' needs and staying focused on a common cause. These are all examples of natural communities of practice. The goal of the smart manager is to create similar types of communities where they do not yet exist. In a knowledge driven organization these communities must be formally created and managed until such time that they become second nature.

But how do you do that? Provide for the group a sense or need to :

- *share*

- *cooperate*

- *focus on a common goal.*

Of these, perhaps the hardest to instill is a need to share what you know. For most individuals, this goes against virtually everything they have been taught since their first day at school. From academia to professional life, it is what YOU know that separates you from the rest, and is the foundation of how you are valued. Some feel a threat in surrendering their knowledge, in fear of making themselves obsolete. This must be dealt with head-on. (See Chapter 2 for more detail on handling the threat to specialists.) But, in addition to educating teams on the value of their contributions, individuals often need real concrete evidence that cooperation and sharing are not only good for the common goal, but for themselves. This is the focus of incentivization plans, which are discussed in more detail later in this chapter.

There are no magic answers on how to instill these priorities in communities, but certain tenets should be heeded. First, you must deliver a clear and consistent message to the general community that knowledge sharing is a serious direction of the organization, and one that high value has been placed on. Then demonstrate the value of knowledge sharing (see the discussion on incentivization below). Second, look for existing informal communities of practice and other cultural queues that you can leverage and transform into knowledge communities. (The knowledge audit should help uncover these.) Hold informal meetings (i.e. brown-bag lunches, etc.) to continuously nurture and reinforce the communities.

In addition to educating teams on the value of their contributions, individuals often need real concrete evidence that cooperation and sharing are not only good for the common goal, but for themselves. After all, if the half-life of knowledge is constantly being reduced, the value of what anyone knows is worth less and less every day. Why not use this knowledge in trade for new knowledge? If knowledge has value, it is subject to the same economic factors that any other form of currency is – namely the time value of money. A difficult concept to grasp at first but vital to survival in a knowledge-based world and economy.

Ultimately, it is the promise of personal advancement that is the focus of incentivization plans. The objective is simple, incentivization should be based on reciprocity, not just individual compensation. The latter will lead to the erosion of trust and the destruction of communities. Establishing the former, however, is a matter of demonstrating the compound benefits of a one-to-many relationship. Simply put: I am one of many in the community; if I give once, I can take many times over. It is this belief that will build a sustainable knowledge-sharing community. And it is this type of personality that will pervade the competitive landscape of tomorrow's knowledge-based organizations.

The ownership of knowledge

A word of caution must be stated with regards to the approach to managing knowledge. Indeed, many have challenged the phrase knowledge management itself. If knowledge exists in the minds of those that use it, how can it be managed? Management implies control and external possession.

Smart answers to tough questions

Q: If I surrender everything that I know, do I not obsolesce myself in the organization?

A: No, your greatest value is not what you know, but your ability to keep pace with new knowledge and the intellect that forms your ability to learn. That intellect does not diminish. The organization will not find you obsolete because it now knows what you know. Remember, the half-life of knowledge is ever decreasing. The irony is that you must constantly unlearn and re-learn in order to be valuable. Your value and that of your organization is fundamentally your ability to selectively let go of what you know and continuously innovate.

A smart manager will readily agree that knowledge cannot be managed. You will not, however, get hung-up by semantics. In spite of what it may be called, you know that the goal of knowledge management is to foster the sharing and leveraging of a collective knowledge base, not to take possession of it. Foster this idea in your community. Explain that knowledge will not be managed but cultivated. Demonstrate the reality of the approach you intend to "manage" knowledge. This can be done via the approaches taken to incentivization and leadership style. The task of knowledge leadership may, ultimately, not be so much to manage, as it is to form agreement on the practices and methods by which the value of knowledge is interpreted.

Incentivization

The issue of Incentivization has been alluded to throughout this book. Perhaps this speaks to the pervasive nature of this challenge. In Chapter 2 we discussed the reluctance of some specialists to share their knowledge. Many people often have difficulty in releasing their content. They're very proprietary about it. You may create a great platform, great design and all the standards that you need to support the sharing of knowledge, but you still need to provide incentive to the individual lines of business, and to individual employees to use the system. The knowledge base must be constantly updated as new knowledge is acquired.

In Chapter 3 we introduced the dilemma of organization, which focuses on the disconnection with regard to storing knowledge, between the knowledge provider and the knowledge seeker.

The dilemma of incentivization is related, but is much more culturally oriented. In building a knowledge sharing community, there still needs to exist an onus for wanting to share knowledge. In the pharmaceutical company introduced above, for example, there existed a very strong knowledge-sharing culture. Individuals used words such as "family" and "united cause" when speaking of their relationship with co-workers. Knowledge was freely shared. You may think that this organization had few problems to overcome with regards to sharing. But this conclusion is short-sighted.

In this organization, despite the willingness to share, there was no incentive to do so. Sharing occurred if and when a co-worker asked for knowledge. But, despite the creation of elaborate knowledge-based systems, virtually no one was taking the time nor making the effort to formally store their knowledge into these systems to promote wide scale accessability. The reasons for this were not based in a tendency to hoard, but rather a lack of reason to make this extra effort. Employees did not see knowledge-sharing as part of their formal job description, did not see management recognizing it as part of the work effort, did not feel they were recognized for doing it. Therefore, while from a cultural and personal standpoint employees were all willing to share what they knew, in a formal capacity it wasn't happening.

The issue of incentivization derives from the fact that the knowledge seeker is the recipient of knowledge that will empower him/her to perform useful functions, and is thus keen to receive the knowledge. On the other hand, the knowledge provider usually sees little benefit in sharing the knowledge. At best, this requires effort on the part of the knowledge-provider that could better be spent more productively on his/her own projects. The knowledge-seeker's need for the knowledge is hardly an incentive to the knowledge-provider to share knowledge. In a worse scenario, the knowledge-holder may choose not to share knowledge, as it is a source of power to its owner (albeit a short term source of power given the half-life issues we have already discussed).

How, then, can the knowledge provider be incentivized to share this knowledge? The answer lies in two basic approaches, metric and method. A smart manager knows that a carefully tailored plan for each must be constructed prior to attempting to roll out a knowledge management system.

Metric

We should state at the outset that the metric side of the equation gets a fair amount of criticism since it begins to resemble a "big brother" view of the organization if it is used in an oppressive manner. But metrics can play a significant role in incentivizing knowledge sharing.

Knowledge metrics refer to how your organization recognizes that knowledge-sharing has occurred. Until your metric is well defined, to the point where it can be communicated and easily understood throughout your organization, any attempts at defining a method can prove futile. Look at this as a means to recognize people for their efforts in sharing knowledge and in advertising the success of knowledge management to the rest of the organization – the nay-sayers.

First and foremost, individuals need to know what constitutes a knowledge-transfer or -sharing. There are at least three popular techniques that you can choose from – in our experience only one is likely to help:

> *Smart quotes*
>
> What gets measured is what gets done.
>
> Anon.

- *Input* – If a formalized repository has been created for the capture of knowledge, a process can be put in place that would record the occurrence of each input. Thus, knowledge-sharing could be measured by the frequency of input to the system. Smart managers will shy away from this approach as it fails to take into consideration the full cycle of knowledge-transfer. In this scenario, the knowledge-seeker is not taken into consideration. Therefore, you run the risk of incentivizing the input of useless information. Users may be apt to contribute virtually anything in order to be recognized as a sharer. In fact, we know of a situation where a senior knowledge worker at IBM once reconstituted a co-worker's document and submitted it in order to gain credit for contribution to a knowledge-management system, in which contribution was measured in this way. You should place greater focus on the value of the knowledge.

- *Output* – Stress can be placed not just on supplying knowledge – but on being an active participant in the knowledge-sharing process, by being a user of the knowledge as well. In this approach, recognition is given for repurposing existing knowledge to promote new ideas, processes and/or products. While this approach has merit, it does not incentivize individuals to share what they know, just reuse what others have shared.

- *Input/output cycles* – The best way to focus on the value of the knowledge and its use in creating interaction and collaboration is to recognize knowledge-sharing as a complete cycle. Users are recognized not simply for contributing knowledge into a system, but for inputting knowledge that is subsequently used by other individuals. In this scenario, recognition may also go to the user of the knowledge. This sends a clear message that the valuable knowledge worker is not just a provider, but an innovative user of knowledge, which will typically result in the generation of new knowledge. A good way to visualize this is by drawing a large circle with each provider/seeker of knowledge as a dot on the perimeter of the circle. Then imagine lines that connect the dots based on the volume of interactions (consider doing this by analyzing network traffic or e-mail volume). The result would be a real-time organization chart that portrays the communities of practice in the enterprise and identifies the way knowledge is shared. You could then go one step further to identify communities that have been especially innovative and successful as a result of their knowledge sharing.

Whatever approach you take, it's especially important to consider recognizing knowledge-sharing in the context of communities. This helps to create bonds of trust, challenges the individual belief of knowledge as power by encouraging community sharing, and creates benchmarks for knowledge sharing that can be emulated by other communities within the enterprise.

Method

Once a metric is established and clearly understood throughout the organization, the smart manager will establish a method of incentivization. In other words, why would the users want to be recognized under the metric plan? Some not-so-smart managers feel the answer to this question is simple – pay them. But a smart manager knows, money is not always the answer. The method of incentivization must be customized to meet each organization's needs, both those of management and end-users.

KILLER QUESTIONS

To what extent is learning and teaching reflected in your corporate goals, individual goals?

A popular approach to dealing with incentivization is the importance of creating a group…that can help people to find …very self-centered reasons for sharing *knowledge*. The following are suggestions from knowledge leaders in several organizations that have championed Knowledge Management in their organizations.

Jan Scites, AT&T
I know that we have tried very hard in the last year to cross-pollinate. And the best way to get people convinced is to go to their bottom line. The other thing it does is it allow you to normalize – that's one of the models we're using – normalize a high performer from a low performer. So you are in essence capturing what all high-performers do, which is then available to all performers to look at. And it gives us the consistency of running our business, which is fabulous and protects that information so we're no longer an environment of storytellers. The idea was that if a transaction took nine minutes for a lower performer, and a high performer did it in three, we were trying to close it to a two-minute gap between them.

There is an inherent, but unexpected, incentive to this that Brad Meyer talked about.

Brad Meyer, Collaboration Ltd:
Essentially, help people find their own reasons and then their own ways to help themselves (and each other) more effectively. We are asking questions like: "Why on earth would you want to make what you know available to others? I mean, who is there out there that could benefit from your experience in a way that might actually benefit you too? Whose experiences could you yourself benefit from? And when did the last crazy idea come to you from 'left field' that really saved the day? What circumstances enabled that to happen? I mean … how valuable could this be for you personally, if there were some ways that everyone could be really leveraging each other's information and ideas?"

And in response, we are experimenting with a number of ways to draw more deeply from the growing well of our collective experiences. We are finding ways to increase both the quality and the frequency of people interacting and sharing what they know.

One of the ways we are doing this is by using desktop video conferencing. When I meet somebody for the first time and talk to them about the possibility of their taking up the opportunity to use this stuff, they might say, "Well, I'm not sure I really like this because it means that I might become redundant, because they could always use the expertise of somebody in another country who's cheaper." Behind every strong objection is a really strong set of values and beliefs. So in this case, what I might do is ask them, "Hmm so ... if anyone from anywhere in the world could tap your expertise at any time this way ... does that mean you're marketable world-wide now?" Strong objections are great because that means we can then explore them in terms of how you're managing to leverage others' knowledge more effectively, your sharing your own discoveries more frequently can actually help you.

One of the experiments in the knowledge-management world is to have the original – theoretically the original – authors' names attached to a piece of information. It just stays with them for life. Similarly, people who develop a framework or a process which is adapted by others can find ways to stay connected to how many times that's replicated and used elsewhere. People focus on different things, when it comes to receiving recognition. The trick is to identify it, respect it and leverage it.

Rob Patzig:
... we are starting to ask for justification for every business decision an executive makes at any given moment. But if a decision is proven after the fact to have been a bad decision, and there's evidence that the information showing that that was a bad decision was there prior to the decision, chances are you're no longer working here.

(Excerpted from Delphi's Best Practices in Knowledge Leadership)

Many methods have been tried. Many have worked. Many have failed. You must shape the incentive to match the expectations of the users, the culture of the organization and the boundaries of management. Keep in mind that virtually all of these methods can be fitted to a community approach rather than an individual incentive. We favor the former, but again your culture will dictate where to start.

Smart ideas for incentivization

- *Link it to performance/project reviews* – Many users have observed that while management may dictate the need for knowledge management, they do little to make it part of the daily routine. Show users that management is watching and recognizing their positive knowledge-sharing habits by making knowledge sharing part of a formalized performance review. Make knowledge-performance part of the equation on which promotions are based.

- *Awards or plaques*– Often simple recognition of a job well done is enough to motivate workers. This is especially true in organizations that have a strong culture towards personal esteem. In organizations such as this, the awards can carry little monetary value – the proverbial gold watch is not needed, but rather a plaque or mention in a corporate newsletter, recognizing knowledge leaders in the organization. There is evidence that in some organizations, something as simple as preserving the individual identity of an author(s) can have impact on the willingness to share. For example, we are aware of one company that allowed individuals to create individual web pages on the company intranet. This created an internal market dynamic. Over time knowledge workers felt that if they didn't have an individual web page they were not putting their value on display.

- *Time* – Somewhat related to the performance link, employees who work in a production-oriented/nose-to-the-grindstone culture, often point to being given official time to impart what they know, and/or search for what others know, as all the incentive they need to use the system. After completion of a project, for example, perhaps key team members should be given 2–3 days (maybe off site) to formalize what they have learned and externalize that into a knowledge system, rather than immediately being expected to start on another project.

- *Money/prizes/remuneration* – While you may eschew direct monetary reward as a means of incentivization, in some instances it can work, it just is not always necessary. This is particularly true in cases where you need to jump-start an initiative. The most critical aspect of this approach is that it demonstrates in clear terms management's commitment to knowledge management. In some organizations, rather than cash bonuses, contest-like programs were used. The top 10 knowledge-sharers (defined via the corporate metric) receive an all expense vacation to Hawaii, a gold watch, etc.

A smart manager knows, however, that no matter what the metric and method of incentivization is, first and foremost you need to focus on minimizing the burden placed on the knowledge-sharer and -seeker alike. In the former case, this implies the strategic utilization of externalization tools that automate and simplify knowledge-classification. Additionally, profiles of knowledge-providers should be automatically created and maintained to "broker" knowledge providers' tacit knowledge potential. Tools should be deployed in a pull mode (i.e. suck the knowledge into the system as part of the knowledge-providers performing their day-to-day jobs), as opposed to a push mode (i.e. the knowledge provider is forced to separately enter their knowledge into a system). Similarly, employees are more apt to leverage existing knowledge, if the knowledge-discovery process is simple/transparent. Agent technology that matches work being done to known knowledge sources and routes the knowledge to the knowledge worker/seeker can be powerfully aggressive in getting users to proactively reuse knowledge in innovative ways.

The smart manager will also strive to eliminate wasted effort. If knowledge-capture and -classification is a burden for the knowledge provider, performing these functions for knowledge that is not used later is adding insult to injury. Wherever possible, defer capture and classification processes until after a need for the knowledge has been established. This may mean that only pointers to knowledge sources are captured initially; then, when knowledge seekers require further knowledge, they track the source of the knowledge and "pull" it from the source directly.

Smart quotes

The very essence of leadership is that you have to have a vision.

Theodore Hesburgh

Lastly you must recognize that knowledge seekers and providers alike need a champion. The champion is someone who is responsible for motivating them to participate in the system, to ensure the value of the system and advance the causes of knowledge sharing in the organization. But, this role of leadership is a constant source of frustration. Why? Because, knowledge exists primarily in customer situations, product situations, project situations, and in processes.

If you try to manage knowledge at a higher level of abstraction, at an executive level for instance, you are trying to map an old, very conservative model to the knowledge-management process. At this level, the knowledge is too significantly removed from where the knowledge is generated and captured. Part of a smart manager's approach to knowledge management must recognize this, and therefore not attempt to, in the name of management, shackle users with strict security schemes and rules. The smart manager must leverage existing wisdom in a diffused environment. The knowledge process must stay at the line of business. This is very much dependent on the style of leadership and control that is imposed on the knowledge-management solution in your organization. The various approaches to leadership in a knowledge application is the focus of the next chapter of this book.

The Bastille: a case study

Of all the places you would expect to find knowledge management at work, your local police station would not be likely to come at the top of the list. Yet the problem of sharing, incentivizing, and deploying knowledge management is not a problem peculiar to any one industry. Even in those cases where competitive advantage may not play a role or where innovation is hardly a key criterion for success, knowledge management is becoming essential. The reasons run across industries and through our very social fabric. We are living in an era of ever-increasing globalization, mobility, and connectivity. Knowledge management is not just a capitalist tool for advantage. It is a tool for survival.

Addressing the compelling need for knowledge-based systems in the area of law enforcement has become a critical factor for successful prosecution of criminals. In a mobile society, crime investigation becomes a knowledge-management problem, rendering traditional crime-fighting techniques that focused on the behavior of 'local' criminals virtually useless. Pressure from advocacy groups, local law enforcement, vigilantism, and technology literate constituents has mandated a new approach to law enforcement. This is the basis for The Bastille[SM].

The case study of the Bastille is a lesson in overcoming three important challenges:

- the complexities many organizations will face as they try to cobble together their own knowledge-management solution from new and existing technology components

- the dilemmas of organization and incentivization

- building a knowledge repository of sufficient mass to encourage its use.

The Bastille is intended for users as large as InterPol or the FBI, and as small as the sheriff in Mayberry. It is equally accessible to both because the front-end is browser-based, and the knowledge base is hosted on the network, eliminating much of the support overhead that has been an obstacle to the introduction of automated records management systems in smaller police agencies. The Bastille provides a means of linking together the knowledge resources of large and small police agencies into a single knowledge base. This is a critical capability of the system, because knowledge sharing among police agencies is not the high-tech wonder that Hollywood would have us believe.

Background: the changing nature of crime

The nature of crime – and criminals – has changed greatly as the nature of our society has changed. The increased mobility of society in general is reflected today in the pattern of crimes and the behavior of those who commit the crimes. As recently as 10–15 years ago, crime was still a local problem; a burglar worked in a single geographic area. Repeat offenders tended to commit their crimes under the watch of a single jurisdiction where all of the case knowledge was collected and analyzed by a police team familiar with the case and other cases like it. When crime was a local problem, managing the knowledge to solve those crimes was a local problem too.

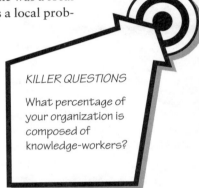

KILLER QUESTIONS

What percentage of your organization is composed of knowledge-workers?

Crime is no longer just a local concern. Today, a criminal might burglarize a series of homes in Boston and then, sensing the heat as the police become more and more focused on solving this spree, move on to another jurisdiction. Suppose he or she moves down the road to Hartford and starts another string of burglaries there. As far as the Boston police know, their burglaries have stopped. As far as the Hartford police know, they have their own unique string of burglaries to solve. Same burglar, different jurisdiction – how will the police know that this is more than a pattern of local burglaries? Suppose the Hartford police arrest our mobile burglar. How will they ever know to link him to the burglaries in Boston? How will the Boston police ever find out their suspect is behind bars? What might Boston have known that could have helped Hartford catch this burglar sooner?

Hollywood had shaped much of our understanding of law enforcement's use of technology. In the movies, it seems as if the police always have instant access to computer records that lead to the uncovering of the identity of the criminals they seek. All they have to do is type a name into a database, or scan in a photo from a crime scene, and out comes a computer-matched identification of their suspect. But like most stories with a Hollywood slant, the reality falls far short of the fantasy. The true heroes of crime fighting do not have it so easy.

In 1996, few people knew about or were talking about knowledge management, and few of the ones who did know about it were building applications to support it. As with the vast majority of knowledge-management applications, the Bastille was not conceived of as a knowledge-management application. Instead it was seen as an application that would deliver a specific solution. The vision was for the sort of crime-information management that David Watkins, chief architect at GTE for the development of the Bastille, and the rest of us had seen the likes of Sandra Bullock using in the movies ('The Net'). In other words, it was conceived as a way to address a particular point-of-pain.

The system evolved from David Watkins' revelation, and was implemented by a small team of developers and knowledge experts. The team included Brian Plotkin, now the Operations Manager responsible for the day to day management of The Bastille. A self-described technology geek, Brian's role in the early stages of the project was that of an evangelist.

Q: *How does it feel to be an evangelist?*

A: *It feels ... different, but it feels good to feel good about something like this. When I first got into this project, I sometimes felt like I was working on some "big brother" initiative, but I realized that we could do something really important with this application, something that could help others. I thought about my own kids ... what if there were some-*

one out there hurting children and this system helped to catch that person? I'd be doing something positive ... working on this project has been hard for an introvert like me, but I kind of got dragged out of it [being an introvert].

Not for the faint of heart

Building a complex knowledge-application like The Bastille is not for the faint of heart. The initial systems analysis proved that The Bastille would not be a single, monolithic application. Instead, it is an application made from a "patchwork of technologies." This is typical of knowledge-management applications.

There are lessons to be learned in looking at how such an application comes together, lessons that are relevant for anyone trying to integrate today's knowledge-based tools into an existing infrastructure of technology. Brian shared his thoughts on the complexity of the problem and their approach to the various problems:

Smart quotes

Diffused knowledge immortalizes itself.

Vindiciae Gallicae

Q: *Tell us about the different components – what went into the creation of this application?*

A: *We knew early on that we were not going to build the entire application ourselves. We wrote the underlying infrastructure, process-flow functions, and the basic interface ourselves. We put the rest of this together by selecting various technologies and then asking the vendors to make them work together.*

Q: *What was that like – what kinds of challenges does that represent?*

A: *You have got to look at your vendors as partners. We needed all our technologies to be integrated, and we needed all the vendors to understand that was an absolute requirement. We started by getting them all together in the same room and asked them to explain to each other what they saw as their respective roles in the project.*

Q: *What advice would you give others who are embarking on a complex integration effort such as yours?*

A: *First, be up-front. Don't hide problems, make sure everyone knows who else is involved, and play nice. Once you bring the vendors together, get out of the middle and make them resolve their differences and issues.*

Second, communicate, communicate, communicate ... Everyone has to know everything – both problems and successes. There is no such thing as too much communication.

There is no silver-bullet knowledge management solution. In many cases, your solution will consist of existing technology, used in a new way, per-

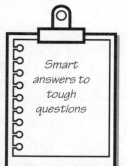

Smart
answers to
tough
questions

Q: If we broker knowledge-people resources, won't the productivity of our keenest individuals suffer from the constant bombardment of questions and requests for input?
A: It depends on how you measure productivity. In a short-term view, yes; but thinking long-term and strategically, no. The goal of knowledge management is to allow the knowledge and talents of individuals to have a broad effect on the organization. By involving these individuals more often, you achieve the benefit of their expertise in more situations, and the spreading of their know-how to more individuals.

haps through the introduction of a new knowledge retrieval application that leverages an existing knowledge repository such as a document management system.

Think locally, act globally: a knowledge-sharing approach for police

The knowledge-management problem in law enforcement

Computer automation of police record systems is a classic case of "have and have not." Here is a case where size does matter – the larger police agencies have the resources to develop systems of their own, but the smaller ones do not. Charlie Gray is a systems engineer for the Brevard County (FL) Sheriff's Department, ranked in the top ten largest counties of 69 in the State of Florida. Charlie says the first priority for knowledge capture, for his and other county agencies, is to improve the collection and assimilation of knowledge within the county. A second clear priority is to share their knowledge with others, but this priority takes a back seat in many agencies because they do not have their own house in order.

Charlie described a poll he conducted with 115 police agencies in Florida:

We asked these agencies to rank their top three requirements for record automation.

KILLER QUESTIONS

If a junior staff member has a good idea, what is its likely outcome?

- *The number-one answer was the need to share information within geographically adjacent areas (e.g. adjoining counties).*

- *The number-two answer was the need to distribute information on non-felony warrants (felony warrants are already widely distributed).*

- *The third was the need to track mobile criminals, to know when a criminal has moved into another area and to share what agencies in other areas know about that criminal's behavior and methods.*

These survey responses are not surprising; they reflect the fact that knowledge-sharing starts as a centrally focused problem but then spreads concentrically outward as the more immediate needs are resolved. As a practical matter, they can all be addressed by a knowledge-sharing application like The Bastille, but this application faces two dilemmas that all knowledge repository applications face – how to populate the repository and how to encourage others to use it.

In the dilemma of organization, the knowledge-provider struggles with the problem of how to organize the vast amounts of knowledge that he has to offer, not always knowing in advance how the knowledge-seeker intends to use that knowledge. Large agencies like the Brevard County Sheriff's Department face the dilemma of organization, and they view The Bastille as a solution to that dilemma. Brevard has its own automated records management system in place, a system that they rely on within the county for crime knowledge management.

Because they have a sophisticated record-management system, Brevard is frequently called upon to share their knowledge with other agencies throughout Florida. Today, they do this by telephone, using expensive staff time to answer calls, perform searches, and generate replies. Telephone inquiries are, by definition, unstructured knowledge requests, and part of the challenge to providing a response is to first resolve what is the actual knowledge request.

Brevard County intends to use The Bastille as a means to share their vast knowledge base. Using a customized interface, Brevard will feed knowledge from their crime records management system into The Bastille automatically, where that knowledge will then be available in The Bastille's standardized format for other subscribers to use. The benefit to Brevard is that by providing this knowledge directly to a larger knowledge repository, other agencies they support today will have another means to access that knowledge, along with knowledge shared by other police agencies. This frees up the time currently spent by Brevard County staff in answering the knowledge requests from other agencies.

Incentivizing knowledge-sharing

It is clear that Brevard County has an incentive to share their knowledge, and The Bastille facility addresses their need to organize it in a familiar way. But there is another issue that they face related to knowledge-sharing incentives. Brevard can also benefit from the shared knowledge of other County agencies, but not every agency is in a position to provide this knowledge in the same manner as Brevard County. Charlie explained it this way:

Q: *Will you have access to knowledge from the smaller counties?*

A: *I don't know how the smaller counties will ever be more than just users of the system. They don't have automated crime record management systems of their own that they can feed information from, so in order to contribute to the system, they will have to manually enter their crime information through The Bastille interface.*

Q: *Well, could they use The Bastille as their records management system?*

A: *They could, but most of them don't have the resources to pay someone to do the basic data entry. They still rely on paper incident logs and other reports to track their crime information. Simply put, they are not going to have the staff-hours available to do this kind of entry in any consistent manner. At most, they will be able to find the time to use it when they are investigating a crime, but I don't expect that I'll see good information from them in the system.*

From this, it appears there is a wide resource gap between knowledge-providers and knowledge-seekers – if you have resources, you have a records-management system already and you can be a net contributor to the shared knowledge repository. If you have no resources, you can benefit from others' contributions but cannot contribute on your own. Obviously, Brevard County would benefit from access to knowledge contributed from all of the other 68 counties, but for now they cannot count on those contributions.

This is another manifestation of the incentivization dilemma – unequal contributions by the various users of the application. In new applications, it is often the case that knowledge providers need an incentive to contribute their knowledge to the knowledge repository. It may be that a large user can be incentivized to share simply because a common knowledge repository addresses their need to better organize the knowledge they already share at the same time that it relieves the current demands for access by knowledge-seekers.

But in the case of the small user, even where they may have all good intentions – after all, police agencies are known for their willingness to help other agencies – sentiment is not enough. Intentions and desire do not directly translate into staff-hours, and in a non-profit business, there are limits to an organization's ability to generate the resources it needs to accomplish its work.

The participation by large agencies like Brevard County builds content and provides incentives for other Sheriffs in Florida to sign on as consumers of Brevard's crime knowledge. But for Brevard County to benefit from this application, they will need other counties to at least become contributors in some way, even if they continue to take more from the system than they put in. The answer of how best to do this is not clear.

One solution to incentivization: involve the knowledge-management market-makers

In this case, the dilemma is GTE's problem to solve. The Bastille is a commercial application – subscribers pay GTE for access to the knowledge repository, with its elaborate and powerful retrieval tools. In order to increase the attractiveness of this application, GTE needs to encourage many large agencies to become subscribers and net contributors of knowledge to the knowledge repository.

To date, this has been GTE's approach to building the network. Suzanne Fickes, GTE's Channel Manager for Law Enforcement Services, explained it this way:

Q: How will you build the network of users?

A: [GTE's] approach is to get the bigger agencies to sign-up first. These larger agencies already have a Records Management System (RMS) in place, and we want to make it easy for them to share content from their system. So, for example, we are identifying one large agency in every state for which we will develop an interface to their RMS, free of charge. Once they are onboard and providing data, we expect the availability of that data to attract smaller agencies that already depend on them anyway. This approach is based on the 80/20 principle – 80% of criminal activity knowledge will be provided by 20% of the agencies.

Smart quotes

Unlearning must often take place before learning can begin.

Gary Hamel (author, *Competing for the Future*)

An incentive for smaller agencies: cool tools

For smaller agencies that do not have a RMS of their own, GTE proposes a secondary incentive beyond gaining access to the knowledge provided by larger agencies:

Q: What's the incentive for smaller agencies to put their crime knowledge into the repository?

A: The Bastille is not an RMS, and we are careful not to position it that way. But for smaller agencies that cannot afford an RMS, The Bastille provides a subset of the capabilities found in the traditional RMS. So, they can benefit from accessing other agencies' knowledge, and they get a place to enter their knowledge. If they contribute, they get state-of-the-art technology (e.g., facial search, crime mapping) to apply to their knowledge and others.

A third incentive for the small agency to enter their data is that The Bastille will improve their chances of solving crimes committed in their local jurisdiction. The ability to close a case will be greater if the data is available to other, larger agencies. GTE feels the smaller agencies will supply the resources to enter data that lends itself to identifying the "mobile criminal."

This is as far as the incentives go, at least through 1999. GTE will continue to focus on the first incentive, building the network by attracting the large agencies. While the second incentive – having a place to store local knowledge – sounds rational, it will remain the weaker selling point because it does not address the issue raised by Charlie Gray concerning the availability of resources in the smaller agencies to support the entry of knowledge. The third incentive directly addresses the issue Charlie raised, and while it is a plausible assertion, it has to be proven over time. An early success or two, where a small agency first invests the resources and then solves a local crime because another subscriber had access to their local knowledge, will go a long way towards proving the claim.

KILLER QUESTIONS

Is serendipitous discovery considered an acceptable method of conducting business?

Lessons learned

When crime was a local problem, there was little need to share knowledge about crimes and criminals outside the local jurisdiction, and police agencies never developed knowledge-sharing practices. Now that they need those practices, old ways of sharing knowledge stand in the way. The same could be said for just about any company in any industry.

You can never discount the simple fact that it is exceptionally hard to pry people away from doing what they have always done, especially when the new way is radically different from the old.

Builders of knowledge applications cannot depend on the Field of Dreams phenomenon of "build it and they will come." Every organization developing a knowledge application faces the same fundamental problem – developing critical mass. And here, as in most things, the primary impediment to reaching critical mass is inertia, caused by entrenched practices and a comfort level with doing "business as usual."

The vision of an integrated crime knowledge base is a sound one, but to convince others to join, proponents of The Bastille needed to focus on the same three challenges facing *all* knowledge applications:

- reduce perceived risks by setting correct expectations

- remove the burden and threat of knowledge capture and submission by focussing on the right incentives

- create critical mass by finding early adopters to lead the way.

The other key lesson from this case is that building the application itself can be a complex undertaking. Integrated knowledge applications do not come out of a box – they are assembled from components made by different manufacturers. Getting vendors to play well in the technology sandbox is a necessary, albeit often underachieved, core competency for anyone tackling a knowledge management application.

5

Leading the Knowledge-based Organization

Clearly, if knowledge is to permeate your organization, redefine the manner in which value is measured, change the way in which individuals approach their work, and alter corporate culture forever, there must be an internal champion to lead the knowledge cause.

The role of a knowledge leader has garnered much attention of late. But similar to the larger issue of knowledge management, knowledge leadership is ripe with speculation, hype and confusion. Every smart manager knows that the issue of leadership in the age of knowledge is a critical one. But you also know that defining this role in your organization, and identifying the right individual(s) to fill this role are not straightforward propositions.

Like knowledge itself, knowledge leadership is not about tools and technologies. Knowledge leadership is about the fast-rising influence of a new generation of managers with the task of leveraging the collective mind – the working knowledge of intellectually driven companies. What makes knowledge leadership a slippery issue is the unintentionally elusive nature of these managers. Unlike traditional line-of-business managers, knowledge leaders do not fall neatly into the organization chart. They are often leaders of rogue teams, elusive by title, nomadic in their shifting affiliations within a business and savvy liaisons at the collision of information technology and business solutions. Their position in the hierarchy belies their power. They pass under the organizational radar like a stealth airplane. Yet their ability to leverage the intellectual capital of an enterprise can wield more power than most executives and even many CEOs.

The role models provided by these new managers reset the benchmark for all managers. Ignoring their example is to ignore the essential competitive mandate for the 21st century – the stewardship of intellect and human capital.

However, faced with a cadre of complex human, organizational and technology issues, for which they have little or no precedent to draw on, these new managers are struggling to define a discipline and a community for themselves. In the process they are redefining the rules of what a manager should be.

As far as a CKO goes, it seems almost oxymoronic that we're trying to apply a very industrial-age management concept to what everybody seems to understand is a very information-age business process.

Timothy M. Hickemell (Commonwealth Edison – a Unison Company)

Why are these individuals and their skills essential to the modern enterprise? Consider that companies which would not think twice about having a Chief Financial Officer or Chief Operating Officer, relegate the stewardship of their most important asset (knowledge) to the inexperience and insensitivity of technologists – worse yet the white space of the organization chart. It is in this void, created by the deep division of technology and business strategy, that the true power of an organization resides – power that comes from the ability to connect and rewire the enterprise across its many fragments.

Although many organizations realize that the only remaining competitive factor is knowledge-based innovation, they have been slow to respond by developing the necessary skills and responsibilities in their executive and management ranks. The irony is that few organizations are without the basic intellectual raw material to create these roles. In many cases, the traditional corporate structure squeezes the individuals best suited for the task into the nooks of the enterprise and ultimately out the door.

As a smart manager you must focus on this generation of organizational power brokers who orchestrate these connections. These are people who have had to face and overcome the challenges presented by a new egalitarianism that is emerging as organizations, people, and information become universally connected – organizations where everyone is a free agent; CEO of their own enterprise of one, or, to turn it around, 10,000 CEOs in a single enterprise!

The struggles and successes of these individuals provides a roadmap for the future of management and for every manager today.

SMART MANAGERS ARE KNOWLEDGE FACILITATORS

One of the most daunting issues facing knowledge leaders is how to get those who have knowledge to share it. Often the answer lies in the introduction of a third party to help do the legwork and demonstrate the benefits of knowledge-sharing without burdening or threatening the knowledge owners.

Smart managers at Texas Instruments realize that there is great value in leveraging acquired knowledge throughout the organization. As part of a knowledge-management initiative, it was determined that best practices should be shared. But, how do you codify and communicate something that is by its nature tacit?

Realizing that best practices emerge from the trenches, and that often the developers of these practices are not specifically inclined to proactively share them, smart managers instituted the practice of a third-party facilitator between the 'source' and the 'recipient' of the best practice. Over 130 knowledge facilitators worldwide throughout Texas Instruments continuously search the day-to-day events of running the company and identify existing strengths within the organization. The facilitators capture these best practices, and make them available through a corporate intranet.

Each best practice is codified via a title, a short narrative and contact information for the practice owner (this last piece is especially important when the knowledge is tacit and cannot be fully codified). Additionally, a user can perform a full-text search to locate relevant practices.

Over 300 practices have been documented to date. But perhaps the smartest thing management did was to create a knowledge-sharing culture among the knowledge facilitators themselves. Quarterly forums are held for the facilitators, which allow them to interact and learn from each other's experiences.

Who are these leaders? How do you identify them and nurture them in your organization? Why don't these individuals have clear titles and responsibilities? Why not simply bundle them into the ranks of the now well-touted CKO (Chief Knowledge Officer)? *Because most organizations are as naïve about knowledge leadership today as they were about organizational leadership in the days of Adam Smith.*

It can be argued that knowledge leadership is not new. Managing the knowledge of a process is a requirement in any enterprise, even an enterprise of only one person. However, today, knowledge is not the proprietary property of a few craftsman, masters or executives working within the inner sanctum of an organization. Instead, it is a common property of virtually all workers. Add to this the transient nature of today's workforce, the need to quickly connect and mobilize geographically disbursed teams, the highly technical nature of modern work, and you have an immense demand for greater sophistication in the way knowledge is managed.

The irony here is that knowledge is the most fleeting and temporal of resources. Unlike managing property, equipment and people, knowledge managers cannot point to the value of the object they are managing. Not only is knowledge intangible, it is also immeasurable, at least in terms that can be agreed on as an industry.

Yet, a lack of metrics has not stopped organizations from gathering like moths around this new source of illumination. Neither has it stopped them from investing in tools, practices and expertise to "manage" knowledge. For example, in a 1998 issue of *Information Week*, the role of CKO was touted to reap big rewards and eye-popping salaries. Bank Boston, for example, was recruiting a position noted to be worth $375,000 per year, while a New York Law firm hired a CKO at $500,000 per year. According to the article, the ceiling for CKOs was $750,000 – not bad for a position whose value cannot be measured![1]

Although there are a number of organizations with CKOs in place, these are rare. (Many numbers are touted, but we estimate fewer than 1000 CKOs globally currently.) Many other, lesser known titles, and associated responsibilities are in use in organizations throughout the world to identify and characterize their knowledge leaders. You should consider each of these and determine the approach that is best for you and your organization. This is not a lesson in semantics. You will find that subtle but critical differences in style, value and approach are reflected in these various titles and characterizations. Among these are titles such as knowledge manager, knowledge officer, knowledge architect. Collectively these are referred to as positions of "knowledge leadership."

Knowledge leadership typically includes the responsibility to:

- identify opportunities to promote the value of knowledge management

- communicate best practices

- facilitate the evolution of learning organizations

- provide metrics for assessing the impact of knowledge leadership.

Whatever the role and responsibilities of knowledge leadership, few doubt that it is an essential ingredient of competition in the next millennium.

Types of knowledge leadership

Knowledge leadership represents a broad category of positions and responsibilities from individuals who quite literally fall into the *de facto* position of knowledge manager with no change in title, formal responsibilities or compensation, to highly compensated senior executives who are recruited specifically for the role of CKO.

Although no taxonomy could possibly set forth all of the titles and responsibilities included under this moniker, the following are general categories you should consider:

- knowledge engineer

- knowledge analyst

- knowledge manager

- chief knowledge officer

- knowledge steward.

Knowledge engineer

The knowledge engineer is a leader typically associated with an organization that is taking a very tactical/procedural approach to knowledge management. As the title implies, the knowledge engineer is responsible for converting explicit knowledge to instructions, programs systems and codified applications. The knowledge engineer reduces knowledge-based work to replicable procedures by codifying them. One could make the claim that Fredrick Winslow Taylor was a knowledge engineer. The principal challenge of knowledge-engineering is performing it without outgrowing it. Effectively, the better knowledge engineers codify knowledge, the harder it is for the organization to change when their environment demands it.

Knowledge analyst

This type of knowledge leader is a conduit to best practices. The knowledge analyst is responsible for collecting, organizing and disseminating knowledge, usually on-demand. Knowledge analysts provide knowledge leadership by becoming walking repositories of best practices – a library of how knowledge is and needs to be shared across an organization. The liability, of course, is that knowledge analysts can easily take all of the best practices with them if they leave. There is also a risk that these individuals become so valuable to the immediate constituency they serve, that they are not able to move laterally to other parts of the organization where their skills are equally needed.

Knowledge manager

As the title implies, the knowledge manager is an overseer. This approach to leadership works best in organizations that believe knowledge will primarily be the responsibility of multiple individuals throughout the organization. The knowledge manager is responsible for coordinating the efforts of engineers, architects, and analysts. The knowledge manager is most often required in large organizations in which the number of discrete knowledge-sharing processes risks fragmentation and isolation. The knowledge manager provides the same level of coordination across these as a director of marketing may provide across a number of products. The risk in having knowledge managers is that fiefdoms (albeit large ones) may begin to form around the success of each manager's domain.

Chief knowledge officer (CKO)

The CKO is by far the most well-known title associated with knowledge leadership. This is a very traditional, hierarchical approach to the management of knowledge. The CKO is responsible for enterprise-wide coordination of all knowledge leadership. The CKO typically reports to or is chartered by the CEO. Although it would go to reason that the CKO be part of IT (perhaps reporting to the CIO), this is not often the case. The CKO is not tasked with the infrastructure technology but rather the practice of knowledge leadership. At present the role is almost always a solo performer with little, if any, staff and no immediate line-of-business responsibility. The principal liability of putting a CKO in place is doing it too early. Before a culture of knowledge-sharing, incentives, and the basic precepts of knowledge leadership have been acknowledged by the enterprise, or at least a significant portion of it, the CKO is powerless.

Knowledge steward

The knowledge steward is similar to a knowledge manager. These individuals thrive in organizations that do not view knowledge as a corporate resource that must be managed from the top down. The knowledge steward is responsible for providing minimal but ongoing support to knowledge users in the form of expertise in the tools, practices and methods of knowledge leadership. The steward is in the most precarious and most opportunistic of positions. Usually he or she is an individual who has fallen into the role of helping others to better understand and leverage the power of new technologies and practices in managing knowledge. This could run the gambit from having just read Senge's *Fifth Discipline* or Stewart's *Intellectual Capital* to having attended a recent seminar on the subject of knowledge management tools to simply having a greater appreciation for people in the organization who do or do not communicate well. The term "steward" conveys responsibility and a willingness to guide others yet it is also non-intrusive and the near antithesis of ownership.

Which of these roles is best suited for your organization? The principal determinant is the state of your organization's knowledge-sharing, the level of sponsorship for knowledge leadership and receptivity of its culture today.

In addition to making a determination regarding the type of knowledge leader necessary in your organization, focus in on the manner of practice that the leader should utilize. The following are types of leadership styles or practices found in organizations today:

- the nomad

- the executive

- the specialist/consultant

- the community.

The nomad

This approach to leadership works well in situations where there is low to no executive sponsorship, there is a culture that is receptive to knowledge management and informal sharing of knowledge is the goal of the initiative. The nomad is versed in knowledge-management practices and methods, as the result of experience in one part of the enterprise, and will be tasked with sharing his/her knowledge with other functions. The effect is a walking knowledge-management system. If the nomad(s) demonstrates enough high visible payback, executive level sponsorship will usually follow.

The executive

The executive style fits best in situations where there is overt high-level executive sponsorship, isolated sharing of knowledge and a reluctant culture.

Keen on the competitive benefits of leveraged intellectual capital, the executive often builds the vision and value statement for knowledge leadership. If the crisis to which the executive is responding is impending and obvious, or his/her clout sufficient, the next step is almost always to delegate the execution to a specialist who reports to or is closely affiliated with the executive.

The specialist/consultant

This leadership approach is best suited to environments that have line-of-business sponsorship, isolated or no sharing of knowledge and an undecided culture. Conversant in the tools, practices, methods and applications of knowledge management and knowledge leadership, the specialist may be either an insider or an outsider to the company. Organizations diverge on this point, based on the scope of the knowledge-management initiative and the availability of in-house expertise. Even if nomads exist in the organization, it is often helpful to bring in expertise in the area of best practices across other industries and organizations, as long as an inside influence exists to help guide the specialist.

The community

This leadership style works well in situations where there is high level executive sponsorship, a high degree of knowledge sharing and a receptive culture.

Although difficult to imagine in the context of today's enterprise, institutionalizing knowledge-sharing as part of the community-building process in an organization is the most advanced form of knowledge leadership. If knowledge-sharing is acknowledged as a natural state of affairs in communities of proximity, then the challenge of knowledge leadership is removing distance and instituting immediacy, connectivity, and incentives to take advantage of both. Once this has been done, knowledge leadership becomes part of the standard leadership structure, team, and practices of the enterprise.

CKO vs. other forms of knowledge leadership

The temptation of course is to establish a Chief Knowledge Officer. The title of CKO rose to prominence as quickly as knowledge management itself. But the vision of the CKO seems premature at best. A smart manager will challenge the role of the CKO – not the need for strategic leadership in the realm of knowledge, but under the structure and connotation of a CKO itself. The intent is not to dismiss or diminish the value of a CKO, but to offer balance to the much ballyhooed title by considering alternative, lesser-known approaches to knowledge leadership.

Too many organizations have mistakenly applied a very traditional, hierarchical organizational model to the practice of knowledge leadership. This approach speaks to a command-and-control method of knowledge management. For most, knowledge management doesn't work that way. Having a chief officer of knowledge does make sense, given where knowledge actually resides and the state of sharing and incentivization in most cultures.

There are too many natural points of ownership for knowledge, and trying to roll these up to one point of ownership reflects an old, hierarchical approach. Knowledge is stifled by the mechanics of hierarchy. It is also premature to put in place enterprise stewardship of a process that is still barely accepted and practiced throughout the enterprise. In short, building the right culture must precede the development of right practices.

As a smart manager you recognize that knowledge management is driven by lines of business and people at the extremities of the organization. Therefore, the best you can hope to do is to coordinate the knowledge management process, not to control it. For many organizations, therefore, the CKO is an anomaly – a hierarchical construct applied to what is naturally a diffuse process.

The idea of a CKO rarely maps well to an organization's "knowledge-sharing culture," unless the organization is one that mismanages knowledge or already puts impediments and barriers in the way of sharing knowledge. Part of what seems to be at fault is the speed with which knowledge management has come upon most organizations. Beware of heightened awareness in the top third [of management] of your organization regarding knowledge management. Demand may be building, but an ownership structure that is appropriate for the culture and employees may be lacking. You cannot assume that leadership must come from the top down. Not unlike what a lot of companies did with reengineering. As a result, you miss the boat. You miss an opportunity. You start to push this aside and we move to the next panacea.

Yet, organizations rely on hierarchies in order to protect what they consider valuable corporate assets. A CFO, for instance, is tasked with protecting the physical assets of an enterprise. A reasonable question might be, "Should not the same logic apply to intellectual assets?" After all, today knowledge is universally viewed as an asset (albeit intangible and difficult to measure.) But this also causes debate over ownership of knowledge to surface. Does the CKO or Knowledge Manager own the knowledge? In speaking with Jan Scites, a vice president at AT&T, we learned a valuable perspective on this issue:

Yes, it [knowledge] is an asset of the corporation. It needs to be protected. There has got to be an editing function and some kind of centralized arm. But those who can best create the content and who have the knowledge are often the operating heads or business heads, of the business. And they, therefore, have to own it as part of running their part of the business.

The dichotomy here is evident. The corporation owns the asset, yet the individual (the content owner) owns the knowledge. Therefore you may conclude that knowledge leadership should serve the role of the intermediary who mitigates this dilemma. Knowledge leadership in this capacity would also address another problem that can occur with traditional top down knowledge leadership. With a line-of-business approach, there is a strong likelihood that fragmentation of knowledge will emerge (think silos of knowledge.) The benefit of having a knowledge-leadership function in this scenario can be distilled into one word – continuity – the ability to provide for a consistent story across multiple, discontinuous knowledge workers. Indeed, in speaking with Thomas Brailsford, research manager of knowledge leadership at Hallmark Cards, the idea of story-telling as a critical part of knowledge leadership became evident:

Every time we get a new group of managers in the business unit, we get the same questions, over and over again. We have no corporate memory. They start from scratch. Now, we've researched that. They don't know that. So those are some of the issues that [knowledge leadership] should address.

The most general approach used today for knowledge management is in line of business applications. Because of this, a single knowledge leader, across all lines of business, is a tough sell to the line of business managers. A CIO, on the other hand, who would already be in place, may appear to be more likely responsible for knowledge management if there was an enterprise-wide need for it. After all, CIOs already have ownership of the IT systems throughout all lines of business. However, the CIO is not typically regarded as having the ability (skills, process understanding, etc.) to provide knowledge leadership.

What this leaves is a void in most organizations. In this void, you should look for an evolving new breed of leadership, individuals who have great intimacy and understanding of a particular line of business and who provide leadership by promoting best practices.

Finally, you need to consider the very important role of culture in an organization's knowledge management efforts and its use of knowledge leaders, especially when it comes time to decide on an enterprise position for knowledge leadership (i.e. a CKO). Knowledge leadership feeds off the culture, and the culture, in turn, feeds off the leadership. Both must be evolving and growing towards a firmer grasp of what knowledge management is and how it is instituted. Perhaps most important, both must be synchronized if either is to succeed.

Many organizations have also voiced the opinion that the installation of a "traditional" CKO can send out the wrong message to the organization. The CKO carries with it a sense of layers of unnecessary bureaucracy. This opinion was best espoused by Jim Allen, technical information director at Dow Chemical:

Why do we need [a CKO] – what is the driving issue or burning platform that says we can't [manage knowledge] within the functions we have, if we work in a cooperative way? We're not big on too many layers of management around here. We've downsized, removing organizational layers. And people are not interested in putting in either bureaucratic structures, organizations or loads of specialized people. They might reorganize, but certainly not add huge organizations to help others manage their business. And they know they're going to have to think about it more, but we want to do it as best we can with the structures that we already have in place.

Another fundamental concern associated with specifically putting a CKO into place was the potential for suboptimization; that you may end up with someone whose vision of knowledge management dilutes the effectiveness of managing knowledge in each of the particular business units, projects or teams. These groups need to find out within their area what the best way is for them to manage their knowledge. It is this precise insight that leads the smart manager to focus on the term "knowledge leadership", not CKO specifically.

When interviewing Thomas Brailsford at Hallmark Cards regarding why his organization avoided the use of a CKO, he offered this advice:

A CKO cannot manage knowledge. Knowledge exists with the workers; knowledge is inseparable from the people. Knowledge management is an oxymoron. You can't manage it. And that's one reason we wanted to stay away from knowledge management. We wanted leadership. We felt like leadership was much more appropriate than management. So we've concluded that you cannot separate knowledge creation from the people nor from their jobs. And that learning and acquiring knowledge is an actual by-product of, or is the essence of, a knowledge worker's profession. And so, that is a naturally occurring process throughout your organization. Rather than having a person who can bring all of that together, you need to have a culture, and an infrastructure that facilitates bringing all that stuff together.

Many industry pundits would warn the smart manager that having a CKO sends out the wrong message. The line of business managers have to buy into knowledge management applications for their specific projects, products, and customers. The best that knowledge leaders can do is to create a team or a group of individuals who can help each line of business understand the benefits of sharing knowledge, coach them, and act as stewards of the knowledge-management practices. But the knowledge does not belong to these individuals. They do not control the knowledge. The notion of a CKO carries with it the idea of control. No one person, no one organization, can control all the knowledge across the entire enterprise. It is a hierarchical response to what is not a hierarchical problem.

Kent Greenes at BP, which has been widely publicized as a leader in knowledge-based initiatives due to its CEO's (John Browne) outspoken nature on the subject, describes the approach they use for knowledge leadership as developing an internal capacity in the individual business units:

I spend most of my time engaging the businesses and doing the awareness and stewarding and coaching. We don't do any bit of support unless there is a business champion that says I want to do this, or we influence them or convince him or her to do it, and they own it. In fact, we take it so far as they have to demonstrate that advocacy if they want our help by putting their own business people in a role part-time to be the person who receives and internalizes what we do so that it becomes part of a sustainable capacity in their own team and the organization. So, our main approach is all about creating an internal capacity for this, not at the top, but within each business area. The response has been great. Right now, in our eighty business units, there are about one hundred people who are calling themselves knowledge managers, knowledge guardians, knowledge harvesters, or knowledge coordinators. It does not matter what they are called. When we engage them, we put it in their language and meet them where they are at.

Dow Chemical takes a slightly different approach to knowledge leadership. From this, the smart manager can learn the value of placing knowledge leadership in multiple roles throughout the organization. According to Jim Allen of Dow Chemical:

We do not have a CKO. If I had to guess I don't think we will have a

CKO. We have the human relations resources groups that have certain responsibilities for the development of competencies and how groups can better share and network. The other piece we have is intellectual asset management. Their job is limited to evaluation of intellectual assets and better practices for managing intellectual assets. We have the information systems folks, who are, as we move towards the information-sharing world, the road builders to a large extent. And then the individual business groups, by themselves, have the ultimate responsibility for their knowledge. Those individual core groups have certain competencies or their own business product process competencies. They have specific responsibilities for all their subject matter and knowledge management.

The bottom line, stated once again is that the smart manager should accept the fact that a knowledge leader of one type or another is a requisite of a successful knowledge initiative. But, as a smart manager you should not assume that the title CKO, and the role it connotes, is the best way to provide that leadership. At best, CKOs could be a short-term response that gets organizations started on the solution of a long-term problem. The CKO may be positioned as a temporary evangelist for the organization, but would not obviate the need for other types of knowledge leaders that would be responsible for leading knowledge practices on an ongoing basis. Hybrid approaches are valid. But, in each case, the definition of leadership must be preempted by a careful analysis of user needs, management needs and cultural expectations.

When all is said and done, you should be certain that whoever is selected as a knowledge leader in your organization, he/she exhibits passion for the job. Knowledge leadership is not for the faint of heart. This may seem like a soft issue, but one that should not be dismissed. These individuals have found in themselves, what is today, a unique set of skills, experience, and aptitude. However, this can result in as much frustration as anything else, since these individuals have no one to turn to for a benchmark. They are the role models for their profession. Perhaps that's one reason why so many knowledge leaders tend to work in teams.

So what are the unique qualifications of these impassioned individuals? There is no single profile. But there are some similarities. The most notable are hybrid IT/business experience; at least 10 years (and often much more) of line of business experience; an entrepreneurial attitude and a fair amount of interest in building careers for the future. Knowledge leaders have a keen sense of the business. They have a fundamental, almost instinctive, sense for the way that people and processes function in the enterprise. This is usually the result of extensive first-hand experience. In fact, bringing in an extraordinary experienced CKO is far less desirable than creating knowledge leadership from individuals who understand the business but who lack previous experience in a formal knowledge leadership role.

It should be made clear, however, that an awareness of principles, practices, and tools for knowledge management is a prerequisite for any knowledge leadership position, as is a sincere and visible commitment to knowledge leadership on the part of the organization's CEO. Although typically in a staff capacity, knowledge leadership should have direct access to the CEO and be commissioned through the CEO.

The transformation to knowledge leadership

In the same way that our previous discussion on how knowledge leadership is instituted followed a standard progression through nomad, executive, specialist, and community, an enterprise undergoes a standard transformation as it broadens the scope of its knowledge leadership efforts. This transition has an effect on the ability of an enterprise to not only better share knowledge, but also to better recreate itself as its markets and economics change. Enterprises at the low end of this scale tend to resist change even though they are likely to have the raw material to address sudden shifts in the market. A timely example of positive transformation is Sun Microsystems' ability to reinvent itself with Java, which was in actuality a product that had existed at Sun for nearly five years prior to the advent of the Web. Organizations like Sun are at the high end of this scale, able to quickly use community methods to bring narrow ideas into the mainstream. While companies, such as the former departmental computing king Digital Equipment Corporation couldn't get their good ideas out of a paper bag (and a very thin one at that.)

Here is the evolution and some of the dynamics at play as organizations become more sophisticated in how they manage knowledge. Scrutinize your organization and become familiar with its current stage of evolution. This in turn will help direct decisions regarding the role that knowledge and knowledge leadership can play in your organization.

- individual fiefdoms (centralized knowledge)

- process/product communities (centers of knowledge)

- cross-functional communities (decentralized knowledge)

- enterprise best practices (distributed knowledge)

- the collective (networked knowledge).

Individual fiefdoms (centralized knowledge)

Small groups of functionally related individuals (usually led by one very experienced individual) develop informal approaches to gathering and sharing knowledge. Their challenge is getting it onto the organizational radar screen. The ideas either die or immigrate to better surroundings.

Process/product communities (centers of knowledge)

Groups share project/product-based knowledge in close proximity through interactive methods in order to transfer skills and lessons learned. Better than fiefdoms since the community sharing results in longer memory, but it is not often leveraged across communities.

Cross-functional communities (decentralized knowledge)

Process/project communities form affiliations across the enterprise, which allow for the sharing of experiences and knowledge in predictable format without definite results in mind. Difficult to enforce since the result is indeterminate, but valuable in building empathy and appreciation for benchmark practices in unrelated process/project domains.

Enterprise best practices (distributed knowledge)

If cross-functional communities can survive long enough, their interactions can be institutionalized. Process/project knowledge is captured in a form that allows it to be shared and leveraged across other functions/projects/products.

The collective (networked knowledge)

Best practices are not only captured and shared enterprise-wide, but act as the springboard for a constant stream of hybrid knowledge creation.

In a similar manner, an organization will use various tools and methods during its transformation to transfer and preserve knowledge over time. In assessing the need for and type of knowledge leadership applicable to your organization, ask yourself what types of tools and approaches are in use throughout your organization. The following compares methods and tools that organizations, at different levels of transformation, use to transfer and preserve knowledge over time:

- *immediate*

- *short-term*

- *long-term*

- *institutional.*

Immediate

Completely synchronous exchange. Represents the minute-to-minute transfer of knowledge on an as-needed basis. This can be viewed as the shoulder to shoulder transfer of know-how from one individual to another in close time and space.

Short-term

Usually separated by short intervals of time with no real geographic obstacles. For example, consider a call center where individuals exchange information informally over lunchroom discussion and periodically through team-based instruction. However, lessons learned from a call at 8:05 are not available to another rep at 8:06.

Long-term

The separation is most often due to lengthy lag in time with geography being irrelevant. For instance, the lessons learned by an expert cannot be conveyed to his replacement if the expert is deceased. Geography plays no role in this. It is simply a matter of an immutable time barrier.

Institutional

The most extreme form of time-and-place separation. Institutional knowledge transfer requires that the knowledge be captured and preserved without regard to its time or location of origin and available to anyone without regard to time or place in the future.

Level of transformation			
Immediate	Short term	Long term	Institutional
Fiefdoms			
Individual instruction	Individual observation	Mentoring	None
Process/project communities			
Team-based instruction	Project management	Written procedures	Knowledge engineers
Cross-functional communities			
Knowledge directories	Structured database	Knowledge analysts	Knowledge managers
Enterprise best practices			
Knowledge agents	Knowledge agents, search and retrieval	Distributed knowledge base	CKOs
The collective			
Pre-emptive artificial intelligence	Point of knowledge capture	Networked knowledge base	Knowledge stewards

A final word on leadership

A smart manager should not fall prey to the organizational knee-jerk reaction to most sudden market or economic shifts, namely to assign executive responsibility to guide the enterprise through the new landscape. This is what has caused the onslaught of "C" level officers throughout organizations today. This is especially true of areas so new that skills and competencies in their implementation are lacking among traditional executive ranks.

This does not provide a prescription for adequately leveraging an organization's knowledge. Chief executives fulfill four basic sets of responsibilities. They provide:

- vision

- awareness of purpose

- standardization of best practices

- stewardship.

Vision offers a clearly articulated statement of direction. Every organization needs such a direction if it is to align itself around a common purpose and in a common direction. Vision also shapes the day to day thinking of individuals in such a way that their contributions can be measured against progress towards the vision.

However, vision will not achieve these objectives if it is not communicated. Successful chiefs spend inordinate amounts of time conveying their vision and generating an awareness of purpose for the many constituencies of an organization. Many a vision has been well articulated and understood in the boardroom, only to be lost among the workers and frontline players who must convey it to markets, partners, and ultimately cause it to infiltrate the organization's culture.

With a shared awareness of the vision, the chief must take the time to ensure that best practices on enabling the vision (the tactics) are shared among the many factions of an enterprise. This is the real legwork of any executive. Given the luxury to float above the tactical, the executive has the ability to make connections in an enterprise that would simply not be visible to those in the proverbial trenches.

Finally, when the vision has been achieved, it is the ultimate responsibility and challenge of the chief executive to ensure the succession of vision and continuity of success by seizing stewardship of the organization's best practices.

If each of these four are missing in an organization's knowledge management practices, a CKO may well be the solution. However, most organizations have already identified ownership for at least the first two categories of responsibility. What remains is the need for best practices and stewardship. These are not well suited for hierarchical ownership in the case of knowledge-based practices.

A chief executive (typically a CEO) can clearly convey vision and awareness of purpose. An outstanding case of this is BP's John Browne, whose approach to knowledge leadership has been based on many of the principles espoused in this chapter. However, standardization of best practices requires a degree of intimacy with the process level of the organization that is usually far too tactical for CEOs of even smaller organizations – much less global enterprises. This intimacy was a mandate in most of the participants.

A smart manager knows that knowledge management and knowledge leadership cannot be forced onto an organization, its workers, customers or suppliers. The fit must be natural, almost organic. Old, hierarchical structures, which promote a command-and-control philosophy and single point of ownership over knowledge, are doomed to fail. These are antithetical to the nature of knowledge and the motivations to its creation and sharing. You must constantly remind yourself that knowledge leadership is needed, but its role is to lead through example.

Similarly, the stewardship of these practices, and of the underlying knowledge, must be diffused among many roles and individuals. This is not to say that the specific tools, repositories, and even methods for managing knowledge cannot be shared across a large enterprise. They can and should. However, the way in which these are mapped to a particular part of the enterprise will vary widely. Different discipline processes and market requirements will dictate what value and application knowledge has in each part of the enterprise. If knowledge leadership is not also diffused and able to work in a collective fashion to share practices and steward the evolution of these into the future knowledge, your leadership becomes a one-size-fits-all compromise which ultimately offers little value beyond the informal mechanisms already in place.

Knowledge leaders are educators of best practices, they are stewards of the frameworks that facilitate knowledge creation and sharing, but they are not owners. The owners are the individuals who have the most to gain from knowledge management. Knowledge leadership will build the bridges, organizational executive leadership will build the culture, but it is ultimately the knowledge workers themselves who will build the reasons, their own reasons, to use knowledge management.

Keep your thinking regarding knowledge leadership open and dynamic. The needs of the organization at the outset of a knowledge initiative are likely to be vastly different from its needs after the initiative has turned into common business practice. You must constantly reevaluate the need for and style of leadership necessary to "manage" the knowledge of your organization. In some companies that we have worked with positions of knowledge leadership are considered an interim or stopgap measure, which would get knowledge management to critical mass.

CKO – the knowledge gatekeeper

The need to manage a firm's newest corporate resource has given rise to a new breed of executives skilled in leveraging valuable organizational knowledge: the chief knowledge officer (CKO).

Although CKO jobs often lack well-defined benchmarks, the position is essentially charged with setting strategic policy for an organization's ac-

Smart quotes

The goal should merely be to facilitate the creation, distribution, and use of knowledge by others. Furthermore, the knowledge managers themselves should not imply by their words or actions that they are more knowledgeable than anyone else.

Tom Davenport

quisition and distribution of knowledge and learning, based on the premise that increasing people's capacity to take action will enable them to respond more effectively and efficiently to their customers.

CKOs often have the following objectives:

- assessing the organization's knowledge resources and requirements

- establishing a knowledge management infrastructure

- building a knowledge culture, often through evangelizing throughout the organization

- monitoring the value of knowledge and knowledge management initiatives for the organization.

The focus and responsibilities of CKOs are often reflected in the corporate structure. In some organizations, the CKO reports to the IT Department, or to the Finance Department. In other organizations, the individual heads up a distinctly different department that reports directly to the CEO.

KILLER QUESTIONS

- What is your strategy for knowledge management?
- What do you hope to accomplish by initiating knowledge management in your organization?
- What is the primary business goal you are aiming for in becoming a knowledge-driven enterprise?

Smart people to know: lunch with Peter Drucker

There are few gurus whose actual persona lives up to their popular image. But the darkest part of Drucker's shadow is brighter than the greatest illuminations of most management gurus.

I met Drucker at his understated suburban Claremont home. A tiny ranch set on a tiny lot. As I walked up the short winding path to his house I could see someone working in the front room against a backdrop of books which lined the wall of shelves. Knocking on his front door I was greeted by a thickly accented "Come in," unmistakably Drucker. I pushed the door aside and stepped in.

His wife of 50-plus years, Doris greeted me. I followed her instructions and waited for her husband in the living room. I had not even met Drucker yet I was already somehow at ease with this man who lived in such modest means, yet had a reputation that was anything but modest.

I could hear Drucker shuffling in a back room while I waited. My book *Corporate Instinct* and some papers were set on the living-room coffee table. I took a quick inventory of the room while I waited. One wall was lined with books – still not quite as many as I would have expected – perhaps there was a basement store piled high with the collective management wisdom of the last century. On the other side of the room were a set of sliding glass doors leading to a nicely landscaped backyard and pool.

Drucker appeared dressed in what has become his uniform these days, a brightly colored running suit, plaid shirt (adequately adorned with a pocketful of pens), and very comfortable black running shoes.

After exchanging greetings we walked out to my rented car and drove to lunch. At 89, Drucker is still sharp as a tack. He gave directions to the restaurant with the precision of a drill sergeant. I did all I could not to chuckle when he guided me into the parking space. "A little further. Speed up. Slow down. Just a bit more. Get ready to stop. *Now – stop*." Ours was the only car in the lot.

I soon gathered that the Doctor, as everyone from the maitre d' to the waitress called him, was well known in Claremont.

We sat down and both ordered the day's special, lentil soup and a salad with lobster tail, shrimp, and scallops.

I had provided Drucker with questions in advance, but our conversation was scattered about like a random walk through a magnificent library.

From the cost of retrofitting the Getty museum with more bathrooms to the reasons behind the tragedy at Pearl Harbor, we meandered through a first-hand account of what makes organizations work – and just as often why they don't.

We talked about his experiences at Claremont University, and his eponymous management school of which Drucker is not the least bit boastful. But that is his personality. He speaks of his students at Claremont with the sort of endearment that a grandfather may use to speak of his grandchildren. Each one was brilliant. That is essentially Drucker's manner. He speaks of others and the experiences that surround him but when speaking of himself it is almost always with a fair dose of deprecation.

To truly understand Drucker, you must understand two things: every answer is a history lesson, and the obvious is usually the hardest to see from a distance. Drucker has an advantage in both arenas. First, he has been there. And it's exceedingly difficult to argue with first hand experience. Second, he's studied cause and effect at its origin, not from the distance and inherent hearsay of many decades.

A simple example was our discussion about the success of McDonalds, which we ended up on after talking about the typical number of bathrooms in public buildings. (Don't ask how we got on the topic.)

According to Drucker:

Old Man Kroc once said to me no one understands the success of McDonalds. Our secret is that we have enough bathrooms and we keep them clean. Our customers are mothers with small children – and the children couldn't tell one hamburger from another, but the mothers can tell one john from another.

And the manager of the McDonald's first job is to clean the johns every half hour.

And here I am, all these years, thinking it had something to do with the secret recipe for the sauce they put on a Big Mac.

Here are some of the highlights of my conversation with Peter Drucker along with some of his observations that he shared at a breakfast meeting on knowledge management at a Delphi event in San Diego a few weeks after our lunch.

K: *It appears that the biggest challenge in a K-based society is the issue of free agency. Shouldn't KM keep down turnover? How do you structure an enterprise to retain intellectual capital when all the forces in society are causing intellectual capital to move more rapidly?*

D: *Accept that if there is not enough challenge, people will not stay.*

K: *So is the problem in part that traditional organizational structures cause outright boredom and lack of challenge?*

D: *If you are bored it's your fault. Knowledge managers must manage their careers. In a hierarchical organization its much easier to go places [said with a bit of sarcasm]. It is amazing how many things can be hidden in the old hierarchical organization. The flat org demands much more responsibility from the individual, which I approve of but very few people are prepared for.*

K: *But in a free market a flat org is a more efficient organization, right?*

D: *[A] Catholic bishop in my Claremont class said when asked what was his first crisis, "When I had to make the first decision and I realized there was no one to fall back on." As the speechwriter for the Pope you don't have to make decisions.*

In a flat org you don't have anyone you can go to. So far our schools don't prepare you [for a flat organization].

Whether we can change it in our lifetime I don't know. But I think the job has to be done in post-degree continuing education.

I am trying to get across to the individual knowledge people that they have to take responsibility. Business changes [too] slowly.

It is possible that [money spent on] education from employment institutions already exceeds what is paid for college and university [education] – no one can prove it, but it's true.

K: *If that's true how do companies justify the investment in knowledge management?*

D: *There is nothing more expensive in this business than turnover.*

K: *The dichotomy in what you say is that you speak a great deal of retaining people, yet in your recent books you also speak of the networked society. Isn't that a contradiction?*

D: *Absolute contradictions. I've done a lot of work with non-profits and volunteers. Volunteers do not have to show up next Friday – they don't even have to give you notice.*

K: *So, are they a role model for the knowledge-based business?*

D: *If you start out with the premise that knowledge workers are volunteers; in knowledge work, the means of production is now owned by the knowledge worker. They are mobile, and can work anywhere. They keep their resumes in their bottom drawer. Consequently, they must be managed as volunteers, not as employees. Only the unskilled need the employer more than the employer needs them.*

The change agents will be newcomers from outside. A lot of it will be the way Amazon came in, not from book distribution. [This is one of Drucker's most frequent mantras – innovation most often comes from outside an industry not from inside. Ironic, given that inside is where most of the formal R&D investment is made!]

K: *Do you think the speed of innovation, which has forced this sort of change, is due to technology?*

D: *I think you underrate the change in the workforce. I don't know which is chicken, which is egg. If you look at what came first, the change in the workforce came first with the GI bill of rights. You know Harry Truman was ready to go to college when his father went bankrupt in 1911 – Harry had to take over the farm. All of his life he was disappointed he could not go to college. Yet when the bill of rights came up, the august president of Harvard University, his education advisor, came back and said, "you don't have to worry no one will take advantage of the GI bill." Sixty Percent [of those eligible] did.*

K: *You write in your books that this was one of the turning points for the knowledge age.*

D: *Yes. And this came before the technological revolution.*

Our lunch continued as we meandered through dozens of subjects – what had initially appeared to be a random walk through the history of 20th-century management took purposeful shape as Drucker wove together the disjointed events of a few hundred years into a tapestry of common sense. We ended lunch with a bowl of homemade ice-cream, a double espresso, which I came to know as a mandatory item at the end of his meal, and a discussion of his youth, which was littered with the same sort of first person anecdotes and insights.

D: *I apprenticed in a wool factory founded in 1517. The only reason we didn't use quill pens was because Sir William [the owner] found out he could not get quill pens anymore. He then bought a duck farm to make his own. In 1927 they used double entry bookkeeping. They were the first group of apprentices to have finished secondary education. Everyone else had come to work at age 11.*

My boss told me, "I hired you because I do what Sir William tells me to, but I hope you don't mind my opinion – you are too highly educated."

I would agree with Sir William. Peter Drucker is far too highly educated in the workings of the world for most of us to fully appreciate. In what must be the ultimate test of knowledge management, converting Drucker's tacit knowledge into formula defies what may be the most basic law of human nature – learning through experience. Yet, the wisdom provided by perspective is all too often lost in the excitement of what's *new*. In Drucker's own words, "change must come from the outside." Yet it must be firmly based on the success and the failure of the past.

The following are some more elucidations from our lunch and a subsequent address Peter gave at the knowledge management breakfast we held in San Diego.

Leaders blaze trails, aim their people in the right direction, help them chart unexplored territory. Leaders understand the loose-tight ratio of control, how many boundaries to impose, and the freedom required for followers to seek creative ways to challenge current processes.

Bill Ginnodo (author, *The Power of Empowerment*)

Drucker on the progression to a knowledge-based society

Previously, knowledge was an ornament. Even up to World War II, almost all work was manual or skilled labor. In WWII, out of necessity, through management and training we learned to enable many people to do what in the past only a few people could do – produce high-quality optics, make machine parts, build complex machines. We did this through discipline, through study and conscientious attention to process. These efforts had enormous success, resulting in an improvement in productivity of about three and a half per cent, which is a 50-fold increase over a century.

However, all manual and skilled work is programmed by the task. How should the task itself be done? But that may not be the right question. In contrast, knowledge work is not programmed by the task. Knowledge work is driven by the results. The first question must be: "What is the task?"

Drucker on the knowledge worker

The major cause of dismal productivity is that we have knowledge workers doing work that we did not hire them to do, and which probably does not need to be done at all. Productivity of the knowledge worker begins with asking: "What is the task? What is the job?" Even today, we are too quick to ask how to do the task better, and not consider whether it can be eliminated altogether. Only the knowledge worker himself can answer that, but all too often his job consists of non-essentials.

Eliminating non-essential work is the key to the productivity of the knowledge worker. This is the severe limitation of classical TQM, in that it made perfect work that should never be done at all.

As no two knowledge workers have the same job, each one must define their own job: What should we in this organization hold you accountable for? What contributions and results should you be accountable for over the next 15 months?

The second responsibility of the knowledge worker is to educate us. Every knowledge worker must first be a teacher, creating a wider understanding of his or her knowledge. It is their job to describe to the organization the power and limitations of their area of expertise. The knowledge worker must be clear about what people should know about their area, especially what they can and cannot produce. Ultimately, becoming a learning organization requires first becoming a teaching organization.

Unlike manual or skilled laborers, knowledge workers are paid to know something we don't. You have the knowledge, we don't. In the old labor and skill model in organizations, managers had held most of the jobs of the people they supervised. They came up the ladder, jobs changed slowly, the people at the top knew every job in the plant. They were in a position, through their experiences, to specify the information and knowledge needs for employees.

Today no two career paths are the same; no two experience profiles are the same. Knowledge workers cannot assume their managers know what they do. Thus, it is imperative that the knowledge worker educates his associates as to what his job and knowledge are.

Lastly, the knowledge worker must define his or her information needs. In the past this was a management task, because information was scarce. Today, information is becoming a commodity, and the knowledge worker will have to learn and answer the question "What information do you need to do your job?"

Drucker on renewing knowledge and being innovative

The nature of knowledge is that it makes itself obsolete. On the other hand, skills change very slowly. A stone cutter from the middle ages would recognize and be able to use the tools used today. Under these conditions, it was reasonable to believe that when an apprentice finished training at the age of 16 or 18, he had learned most of what he needed to know about his skill for the rest of his life.

How do you manage change in knowledge work? By organized abandonment – by getting rid of yesterday. Managers must plan for organized abandonment, and manage change. Get rid of yesterday; move onto the new. The new always requires able people, who take change for granted and see it as an opportunity.

Drucker on leadership

Great leaders are too often followed by collapse of the business, because succession is too often ignored. Too often, leaders pick their successors, and they tend to pick carbon copies of themselves, and carbon copies are always weak. Two institutions – the Church and the Military – have endured in part because they do not allow their leaders to select their successors.

Note

1. "Knowledge and Learning Officers Find Big Paydays," *Information Week*, June 15, 1998.

6

What We Don't Know

Of course, as a smart manager you want to know not only the reality of today, but the likely reality of tomorrow. How can you plan for the effects of knowledge management into the next 5–20 years? What are we likely to see from technology? How will business and market models be permanently altered?

Within the near term (i.e. 1–5 years) knowledge management is likely to be shaped by seven trends:

- Knowledge management will be an entry requirement for competition, not a differentiator. Around the world, corporate knowledge levels are increasing to the extent that companies that were previously mere copycats are now major innovators. The Japanese automotive industry is a good example; from making cheap runabouts 20 years ago, they now produce some of the most important automotive innovations in the world. Investments in information technology have largely failed to improve revenues per employee in spite of the magnitude of the investment, because companies were unable to differentiate themselves from their competitors, who were making similar investments. In the same way, since knowledge management is likely to be a major target of investment in companies across entire industries, knowledge management alone will be insufficient to differentiate companies from their competitors. Levels of innovation across entire industries may improve, but this is of little consolation to individual companies that will need to match, or better industry standards of knowledge management investment, merely to be considered a viable player in the market. Pity the company which passes off the opportunity to invest in knowledge management. Its competitors will devour it with knowledge-laden products and services which are better, cheaper, and more useful to customers.

- The greatest challenge of knowledge management will be sharing tacit knowledge. The most difficult objective of knowledge management, and the most valuable contribution it can make, is to enable organizations to share their tacit knowledge more effectively. Tacit knowledge contains the keys to the corporate knowledge kingdom. It is the repository for more complex, powerful and better informed knowledge. By definition, tacit knowledge is difficult to convey to others; for those organizations that are able to do so, their competitors must surmount similarly difficult hurdles to remain abreast. There is no easy shortcut to sharing tacit knowledge – every solution will require commitment and perseverance. Some products and technologies and solutions may provide an edge, but these will not perform a magical transplant of knowledge.

- The primary focus of knowledge efforts beyond knowledge management will be creativity. As companies begin to understand, manage and nurture the knowledge that they have, their focus will inevitably begin to shift away from how the knowledge is captured, organized and disseminated, to how that knowledge is used. The most successful knowledge companies will be those which are well endowed with creativity – an essential driver for innovation. Creativity is the application of knowledge in completely new ways. It requires the organization to break free of the obsolete mental models of the past which describe how organizations should act in specific circumstances. While technology will continue to play a supporting role, this is an inherently human function that cannot be usurped by technology. Smart companies are overhauling their recruitment and compensation systems to ensure that they get the best people and hold on to them. They are also investing in skills development and the construction of "creativity-friendly" environments. Routine work will continue to exist in the organization; however, such roles will increasingly be assumed by technology. For example, workflow products will automate many routine tasks, freeing up process participants to perform those tasks which rely on human ingenuity or insight.

Smart quotes

The pace and nature of change means that everyone must engage in lifelong learning.

Gerald Hoffman (author of *Technology Payoff*)

- Successful companies will leverage their knowledge through decentralized intelligence. The most successful companies in the emerging knowledge-based economy will be those that transplant vast domains of decision-making from the upper echelons of the management hierarchy to the people who perform the work itself. Transporting knowledge to management for decision-making purposes is invariably slow, and knowledge about the specific circumstances is often inaccurate or incomplete by the time it reaches these decision makers. This is aggravated when management is insufficiently informed about the context of decisions – knowledge that is usually available to the area affected by the decision. On the other hand, people with hands-on experience of a particular area have the tacit as well as explicit knowledge and commitment to make decisions involving the work itself. They are able to make faster, and often better informed, decisions. This "decentralization of intelligence" is primarily intended to make companies more responsive to an ever-faster changing environment. In the past, too many organizations have not sensed the damage caused by their outmoded thinking until they have been badly harmed. Those organizations which place knowledge and decision-making power in the hands of workers will remain abreast with the changes occurring in their environment. Decentralized intelligence has another advantage. Those companies which have larger human knowledge bases have a greater opportunity to drive innovation through the quantity and diversity of ideas which inevitably result.

- Knowledge management will give rise to an economy of free agents. Whether by design or not, knowledge is productive only when it resides in people's minds, even though these do not belong to the organization. Companies thus invest time and money to increase the knowledge and skills levels of employees (inevitable expenses if a company is to have a robust knowledge base). In doing so, employees become more valuable to the company, and indeed, to other companies. Fierce competition for quality knowledge holders with attractive skills sets and experience bases can be expected amongst corporations; the services of appropriate knowledge holders will be acquired by companies for enormous fees or a share of the ownership of the enterprise. The increased demand for the experts will result in a more mobile job market and staff contingent. Specialists, while extremely desirable to many corporations in the short term, run the risk of being made redundant when corporate knowledge requirements change. However, generalists will be more valuable in the long run, since their acquired "metaskills" which enable them to adapt their skill sets will be particularly useful in a rapidly changing economy.

- Technology will be a necessary, but insufficient, enabler. The higher the odds, the more sophisticated will be the knowledge-management needs of the company. Technology provides a suite of powerful solutions for the transfer of explicit knowledge within and beyond the organization. Even for tacit knowledge, technology is able to enhance the techniques of knowledge transfer by improving the human-to-human interface. However, technology will be insufficient to apply the knowledge usefully once it has been transferred. Technology will remain an enabler of knowledge management, but without humans to create and use the knowledge, the knowledge itself remains worthless information.

- Knowledge management will beget new rules for strategic competition. The capitalist economy, based on the concept that the key enabler of enterprise was the capital held by an organization, is in for a profound change of emphasis: the most important resource for the enterprise of tomorrow will not be its capital resources, but its knowledge. This means that successful small organizations whose only resource is the intellect of its members will become increasingly common. Entry barriers into many industries will drop, especially as technology reduces the costs of participation in global markets. The number of smaller companies, the innovation which emanates from them, and the number of them which grow into major players as a result of quantum-leap innovations will all contribute to increased intensity of competition for today's mega-corporations, and new rules for that competition. Already, upstarts such as Netscape, AOL and Amazon.com have questioned the traditional logic of their industries, causing established firms to revolutionize their rules for competing. Companies will need to be innovative enough to lead their industries, or at least nimble enough to respond quickly to competitors' innovations.

Beyond knowledge management, you should consider the conversion of knowledge into action. Be smart, look beyond knowledge management to re-evaluate the way in which your organization actually applies its knowledge. Strategize towards a future goal, and set the organization's sights on the next plateau. One such vision is one we have termed corporate instinct. Corporate instinct enables the organization to respond more quickly to environmental change by depending on its understanding of current conditions, rather than a reliance on a corporate memory of how things were done in the past.

Smart quotes

Imagination is more important than knowledge. Knowledge is limited. Imagination encircles the world.

Albert Einstein

Knowledge management is rooted in the idea that mobilizing an organization's intellectual resources is essential in enabling the organization to compete in a world where the previously powerful product differentiators, such as brand loyalty, quality, functionality, and price are now increasingly common. Knowledge management provides your organization with a way of breaking free from rigidly held, yet seldom questioned, suppositions about the competitive touchstones of the past, and exposes you to competitiveness based on innovation. But you should view knowledge management as only a first step. As the pace of change increases, as competition becomes more intense and the array of technological, financial and strategic options available to respond to these competitive forces continues to grow, knowledge management will be insufficient as a glue to manage this change. A new approach is needed.

The most effective way for you to respond to its external business environment is dependent on the rate of change it is experiencing. This change stimulates the organization to manage two characteristics, corporate memory and corporate intelligence. Others are introduced here, with knowledge management interspersed to provide a comparison.

Corporate intelligence refers to your organization's ability to create new responses to new circumstances, based, not on its memory of the past, but on its ability to understand the causes of current circumstances, and to use its insight and reason in generating the most effective response to them. Intelligence is particularly useful where memory is unsuitable to guide thinking in new circumstances; thus, as the business environment changes more and more rapidly, so an organization's reliance on its intelligence increases.

We can thus see how the rate of change in an organization's business environment can determine the most appropriate response to that environment. Why do some organizations handle change more effectively than others? The secret lies in applying the most suitable response given the rate of change in the business environment.

Corporate memory

Corporate memory is your organization's knowledge of, and dependence on, its multitude of past experiences, practices and attitudes. When your organization's environment changes slowly or not at all, your memory can help it to decide how to approach future problems. All the information required to deal with the situation is at hand; it need merely be extracted and re-applied. However, when your environment is changing rapidly and profoundly, memory may serve to mislead your organization, trapping it into a mode of thinking that it believes is applicable, but which in fact does not hold water in the new environment. Thus, the greater the rate of change, the less the organization is able to depend upon its memory.

"Intelligence" is not involved at this point, since there is little decision-making to be done. There is a close mapping between the information required to address the present situation, and that required in previous situations. Processes, strategies and industries that operate at this end of the knowledge continuum gain no competitive advantage from the content of their knowledge. As a result, the driving factors tend to be efficiency and cost.

Corporate memory was widely used as an approach in the more placid business environment of the past. Industries that evolved slowly were able to dedicate themselves to fine-tuning their products and abilities, safe in the knowledge that the rules of the game would remain steadfast. Today, few companies have that assurance, and thus this approach is applicable to but a small number of companies and industries. Some heavily relationship-oriented industries are still dependent on their corporate memory, such as legal firms – here, the nature of the relationship is key to the product, and is not likely to evolve quickly.

Knowledge management

You will recognize when your industry and company begins to experience change. Suddenly the age-old rules that have ensured success for so long, will become insufficient to stop a gradual slide in profitability. The past becomes increasingly less of a mirror for the future, and corporate memory as an approach to dealing with the business environment begins to lose its luster. In fact, it may even inhibit an open-minded willingness to consider alternative approaches. If on the other hand, the pace and extent of change remains moderate, your company can succeed by using the knowledge garnered in the past as a point of departure for new approaches in the future.

Knowledge management supports this decision-making approach, which emphasizes the re-use of previous experiences and practices, with modifications to meet present circumstances. A line of cars, for example, which is no longer selling well may illustrate a shift in consumers' perceptions of the car. While an updated replacement model will need to be technologically and aesthetically more advanced than its predecessor, the manufacturer can rely on some basic truths about the product and its market, truths which have not changed even though consumers' taste for the product has. There is thus a marriage of a knowledge of the past with a fresh approach to the use of that knowledge.

Knowledge management, however, implies that this information must constantly be contrasted with that derived from present circumstances, and the "gaps" filled in by organizational intelligence.

Corporate instinct

Knowledge management has enabled companies to respond to the present by making decisions based partly on a knowledge of its past, and partly on a rational analysis of the future. However, in the most rapidly changing environments, where products, markets and rules change on a month-by-month basis, the knowledge of a centralized group of decision-makers may be too slow to translate intention into action, and may thus be as ineffective as no response at all. Huge new markets can be born very quickly, and die out as suddenly, especially as the market as a whole becomes saturated with sophisticated products and satisfied needs.

If this is your environment, you need to be able to decentralize this knowledge, so that its entire force can be drawn upon by nimble teams tasked with meeting a particular challenge. The only approach that combines intelligence and speed with enough vigor to ensure survival is corporate instinct. Corporate instinct is an organization's sixth sense which enables it to overcome its obsolete memory of the past and to use its decentralized knowledge and decision-making ability to respond instantaneously and effectively to market opportunity, customers, and competition. Corporate instinct is most in evidence in industries where rapid, ongoing change is especially common, such as the industries driven by high technology. But it is beginning to spill into other industries. Corporate instinct is the differentiator between the knowledge enterprise which manages its knowledge, yet is shackled to its past, and the knowing enterprise, which is able to respond to its knowledge and create a new future.

Instinct is far different from intelligence.

- Intelligence or intellect (used interchangeably in our discussion) is the application of knowledge within a specific known context.

- Instinct is the spontaneous application of acquired and latent intelligence to unknown situations with an unspecified context.

Plan for a time (sooner rather than later for some industries) when basing management restructuring on knowledge is no longer enough. The installation of a CKO may all too often be a superficial effort to link disparate sources of information. Knowledge requires more than the conveyance of information. It must also provide the basis for learning and the compounding of learning – that is, the ability to create longer term intelligence and ultimately what we term "instinctive" behaviors.

Corporate instinct certainly embodies knowledge, but is a significant step beyond knowledge management. Corporate instinct will extend knowledge management in two ways:

- It will decrease your organization's dependence on its memory of how things were done in the past, and enhance your organization's ability to respond based on intelligence.

- It will diffuse your organization's intelligence from centralized positions of authority across the entire organization, making this intelligent responsiveness *universal* within your organization – thus responsiveness becomes instinctive.

Change in the business environment need not imply that every business situation/event or sale in your organization is different than the previous one. In fact, in some of the most rapidly changing industries, the processes involved remain consistent from customer to customer. What we mean by environmental change is not the customer-by-customer, day-by-day variations which occur on a microscopic level, but the tectonic shifts occurring on a strategic level – the annulment of previous rules for competition, the evaporation of traditional customer bases, the overturning of technological limitations – and their replacement with completely new markets, products, technologies, and rules for competition.

Twenty years ago the Jeep was a close descendant of the rugged, ubiquitous transport vehicle of World War II. It was driven in difficult terrain and under extreme conditions, by people who were concerned primarily with functionality and not appearance. Since the 1980s, however, a wave of affluent baby boomers have transformed the rules by which Jeep plays. The car's market changed – new customers wanted performance, comfort and aesthetic appeal in a family car that would be driven primarily in an urban environment. The product itself changed into a luxurious, technologically advanced, high-quality recreational vehicle with many luxury-like options. As a result, the rules for competing changed. Jeep now has many competitors – even luxury car provider Mercedes – in a sophisticated, high-end market space. Yet from sale to sale, the process of build-

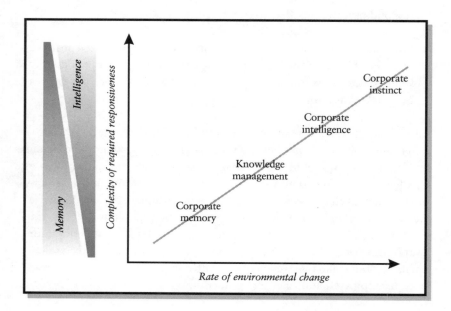

ing, marketing and selling the car remains essentially the same, from car to car.

You should visualize the transition from corporate memory to corporate instinct as different levels on a continuum. The graph above shows how the rate of change in an organization's business environment dictates the type of responsiveness required. The faster the business environment is changing, the more complex the responsiveness required of the organization.

This is analogous to the way organisms have evolved in nature. For squids at the bottom of the ocean, the sea temperature and pressure have remained essentially unchanged for thousands of years. Their prey and their predators, too, are the same. As a result, these big animals have a remarkably simple organic structure – yet one that is well suited to the environment in which they live. On the other hand, humans live in a far more aggressive environment. The land is less hospitable than its marine counterpart; conditions can vary widely within days or even hours – weather, vegetation and topography may change, and (at one stage) wild animals were a constant threat. The human brain was essential in enabling humans to respond effectively to its complex environment.

Smart quotes

The great end of life is not knowledge, but action.

Thomas Henry Huxley

Through the portals

What might the resulting landscape of the knowledge-management industry resemble in 10 years' time when knowledge management has become a standard part of the enterprise IT landscape? One of the most striking ironies is that knowledge will undoubtedly end up the greatest of all organizational assets: likely to be a heated battle ground of intellectual property.

Individuals who become accustomed to this new technology are bound to realize (the smart ones already have) the incredible value knowledge management has, not only to the enterprise, but to their own careers, free agency and, perhaps, even their legacy. After all, intellectual capital is the new wealth asset, and if we live in a knowledge-based society where the factors of production are intellectual, then knowledge management becomes a matter of personal, not just organizational wealth.

In the same way that many a craftsman once brought his own tools to his trade, it is not hard to envision a day when individuals take an ownership interest in their corporate portal tools and bring them along as an essential tool of their trade. After all, their tools, their personally created and customized portals, will be the most tangible form of their knowledge – their structural capital, to use a term popular among the intellectual capitalists we discussed earlier.

What happens when we are brought face to face with unlimited amounts of information and computing power at the same time that the very notion of knowledge as an intangible asset is also being challenged? As with everything of value, accumulation of wealth and the basics of ownership will ultimately play a factor here.

Karl Marx postulated that the economy is the fundamental force behind all human development. "Eras change," wrote Marx in his manifesto *Das Kapital*, "as the factors of production, (technology, resources, and organization) change." He was close.

The radical shift in today's economy is not only in the factors of production, from industrial to informational, but, more importantly, in who owns the factors of production.

Imagine this scenario:, a dimly lit lawyer's office with solemn faces staring blankly across a dark mahogany conference table.

"... to my beloved son, I leave my entire estate except for the knowledge portal which I used to build my expansive fortune. This I leave to my daughter, who I trust will use it to build a better world."

"See sis, I told you dad liked you best ..."

Far-fetched? Only if you discount the value of knowledge management and the ingenuity of knowledge workers in taking ownership over their own destiny – the very mistake Marx made.

Glossary

Agents (Agent Technology) – software programs that transparently execute procedures to support gathering, delivering, categorizing, profiling information or notifying the knowledge-seeker about the existence of or changes in an area of interest.

Asynchronous communication – the ability of two or more individuals in a distributed workforce to accomplish work from different places or different time-modes, via a process intermediary. Knowledge-management tools can perform the work of bridging time and space. In the asynchronous communication model, the process has intelligence to understand the rules and monitoring parameters that must be captured and conveyed to process participants. Asynchronous communication results in a significant reduction in time to resolution since one individual is not waiting for another to perform linear steps in a process. In traditional electronic communications, this is not possible since the process intermediary (e-mail or voice mail, typically) contains no intelligence by which to monitor the work process or communicate its status and prospective impact on other activities.

Business operating system (BOS) – an environment that represents the vast warehouses of knowledge of an organization – the way a business is run, the way people and information come together to add value to a business process. A BOS is a repository comprising a common operating environment, a business process library, and enterprise workflow. The BOS is expressed through a consistent standardized desktop metaphor.

A BOS provides:

- a comprehensive work environment;
- a self-service, reflective desktop;
- a re-usable library-based repository of business objects;
- an open desktop that integrates the business process with any application;
- a constant and consistent interface allowing a process-centric view;
- a clear focus on process functionality rather than applications (e.g., word-processing, spreadsheets, databases);
- a repository for the corporate processes memory.

Cephalic – the approach to decision-making found in command-and-control organizations that route decisions through a central brain or "head."

CKO – see *knowledge leadership*.

Cognition – the ability to synthesize diverse sources of information in making a decision. The aspect of knowledge-management solutions used to facilitate decision-making. As part of a knowledge-map, cognition is the application of knowledge that has been exchanged through intermediation, externalization, and internalization.

Community of practice – communities that form within an organization where people assume roles based on their abilities and skills instead of titles and hierarchical stature. Also referred to as *community of interest*.

Competency management – the ability to use knowledge management to consistently facilitate the formation of new ideas, products, and services that support the core competency of the organization.

Concept-based search – a form of content-based indexing, search and retrieval in which the search-engine possesses a level of intelligence regarding semantics and lexicons. In such a system, internalization and externalization can be achieved at a conceptual level, providing results far beyond that of word-based queries.

Concept-to-cash – the time required to bring a new idea from inception/conception to market. See *knowledge-chain*.

Content mapping – the process of identifying and organizing a high level description of the meaning contained in a collection of electronic documents. Content maps are usually rendered as hierarchical "outlines", but many kinds of more suggestive displays are available through graphical visualization techniques. Content maps are used to facilitate the comprehension of the knowledge base.

Context sensitivity – the ability of a knowledge-management system to provide insight that takes into consideration the contextual nature of a user's request based on history, associations, and subject matter experience.

Contribution monitoring and valuation – a method for analyzing the relative value of an individual's knowledge-supporting activities in a knowledge-management system, utilizing a variety of metrics, which could include the following electronically-based approaches:

- numbers of contributions to knowledge forums;
- numbers of successful problem resolutions associated with an individual's contributions;
- amount of message traffic targeted to take advantage of an individual's expertise, etc.

Contribution valuation need not be technology-based or limited to these specific examples, but it must be grounded in agreed-upon knowledge management metrics.

Core competency – the overriding value statement of an organization. Core competency differs from product and market competency in that an organization's core competency outlives (by a significant margin) product lifecycles and market swings. AT&T's core competency, for example, is connecting people, not telecommunications.

Core rigidity – opposite of Core Competency. Defining any Core Competency too narrowly may turn it into a core rigidity. Core rigidities are unquestioned assumptions about an organization's products, policies, or positioning which lead to complacency and inhibit new innovation.

Corporate amnesia – the loss of collective experience, embedded tacit knowledge, and accumulated skills, usually through excessive downsizing and layoffs.

Corporate instinct – a company's collective "sixth sense". Corporate instinct enables a company to respond instantaneously to market opportunities, customer needs, and competitive maneuvers.

Corporate memory – an unquestioned tacit or explicit understanding of an organization's people, process, or products. Corporations, like individuals, remember the past, including long-standing processes and procedures, along with corporate traditions and values. Memory is strategically important, but it can also become a serious liability if it inhibits an organization from adjusting quickly to its changing environment.

Customer capital – the value, usually not reflected in accounting systems other than as goodwill, resulting from the relationships an organization has built with its customers. One of three forms of intellectual capital as defined by Edvinsson and Stewart. See *structural capital* and *human capital*.

Decephalization – an organization's ability to sense the need for change in its markets and to collaborate in key decisions with its extremities (e.g. employees, customers) and not just its head (command-and-control management). See *cephalic*.

Digital nervous system – the computing infrastructure (desktops, servers, networks, and software) used to inform and support the decision-making processes of an organization. Knowledge management may be part of a digital nervous system.

Dilemma of incentivization – a phenomenon or paradox that arises out of the structural imbalance between knowledge-seekers and knowledge-providers. The knowledge-provider, while able to provide knowledge, typically has little or no incentive to do so. The knowledge-seeker is highly incentivized to receive the knowledge, but is unable to do so without the cooperation of the knowledge-provider. See *dilemma of organization*.

Dilemma of organization (structure) – a phenomenon or paradox that arises out of the asymmetry between knowledge-seekers and knowledge-providers relative to knowledge content. The knowledge-provider is well equipped to provide structure to the knowledge, but typically does not know the context in which it might be used later. The knowledge-seeker is intimately familiar with the context of the required knowledge, but does not understand the knowledge in sufficient depth to organize it or appreciate its structure. See *dilemma of incentivization*.

Disintermediation – the elimination of middle layers of management control and other internal or external intermediaries. The benefit is a faster execution of the knowledge-chain.

Discontinuity of knowledge – a phenomenon that occurs when experienced knowledge-workers move from one position to another position (inside or outside an organization) without having adequate time or knowledge-management facilities to transfer their knowledge to co-workers.

Document management – a software system based on an underlying database, in which unstructured objects (i.e. documents) are indexed and tracked. Document-management systems monitor security, log access to files, and maintain a history of file content. If used to track paper documents, maintenance of content is not provided. Within a knowledge-management system, document management can provide an automated approach to externalization and internalization. In more advanced systems, user profiles can be maintained as objects. In these cases, the owners of tacit knowledge are tracked and made available as a known resource through user queries via *electronic yellow pages*.

Effective engagement – the process by which prospects and customers interact with an organization (customer support, sales, etc.) in a manner that allows for increased customer satisfaction and increased organizational opportunity. Usually facilitated by the use of coaching, problem-resolution, or a knowledge-base system.

Electronic yellow pages – an online listing of personnel, their competencies and their contact information. Within a knowledge-management environment, queries on the profiles will result in a list of known individuals that should possess expert tacit knowledge on the query's subject matter. In heuristic electronic yellow pages the system can infer competencies by observing an individual's behaviors and work product.

Enterprise commerce model – the series of interactions that result from the collision of supply and demand chain activity . This framework provides a compelling argument for the use of corporate portals in building unique value-chain activity.

Enterprise-wide information systems – these systems provide a comprehensive overview of the business and the industry in which the organization competes. An example of such a system is a comprehensive data-warehouse.

Explicit knowledge – one of the two types of knowledge whose taxonomy was most notably espoused by Michael Polanyi. Explicit knowledge is knowledge that is easily codified and conveyed to others. See *tacit knowledge*.

External awareness – the fourth component of the knowledge-chain, which represents an organization's ability to understand the market's perceived value of its products and services as well as the changing directions and requirements of its markets. When coupled with internal awareness, external awareness can lead to the discovery of successful new markets. See *knowledge-chain*.

Externalization – the transfer of knowledge from the minds of its holders to an external repository in the most efficient way possible. Externalization tools help build knowledge maps. They capture and organize incoming bodies of explicit knowledge and create clusters of bodies of knowledge.

External responsiveness – the third component of the knowledge-chain, which emphasizes the perpetual ability to meet the market on its own terms – even when the market cannot articulate these. It is a level of responsiveness to environmental conditions that is significantly faster and based on better connections between resources and markets. See *knowledge-chain*.

Federation – a form of organizational structure where the value-chain is loosely organized as an alliance of independent but reliant organizations or work cells in lieu of departments or divisions within a single enterprise.

Free agency – the lowest level of granularity in a free market workforce. Free agents are effectively organizations of one, which come together temporarily to form project-based alliances.

Generative learning – the additional learning that often accompanies adaptive learning when there is a gap in understanding. Generative learning involves rethinking and redesigning mental models and changing the routes by which individuals adapt to move past where they are to where they aspire to be.

Heuristic software – a software solution that learns about its users and the knowledge they possess, by monitoring the user's interaction with the system. Thus, over time, its ability to provide users with relevant knowledge should improve. See *suggestive software*.

Human capital – the collective value of an organization's know-how. Human capital refers to the value, usually not reflected in accounting systems, which results from the investment an organization must make to recreate the knowledge in its employees. One of three forms of intellectual capital, as defined by Edvinsson and Stewart. See *structural capital* and *customer capital*.

Increasing returns (theory of) – economic theory created by a group of economists (prominently, Brian Arthur and Paul Romer) which proposes that the emerging information-economy, with its shift of value from raw materials and manufactured goods to information itself, requires a new economic model, based on the dynamic of increasing returns of scale. The primary example is the software market, where successful producers (prominently Microsoft) have increasing returns to scale (each new unit of output returns incrementally more profit than the last) because of variable costs approaching zero in volume production, as well as "network externalities," and "lock in." In contrast, in the classical economy, businesses faced inevitably decreasing returns to scale, as successively larger plants eventually reached a point where marginal increases in production required marginal increases in cost.

Instinct – the spontaneous application of acquired and latent intelligence to unknown situations within an unspecified context.

Intellectual capital – can be segmented into three sub-categories: human capital, structural capital, customer capital. Although acknowledged as valuable in most organizations, these assets are not measured and accounted for in an organization's financial statements other than as goodwill. Many believe these assets form the basis for most equity-market valuations of an organization.

Intermediation – the brokerage function which brings together knowledge-seekers (questions) with knowledge-providers (answers). Intermediation technologies facilitate the connections between people and the communication of knowledge between seeker and provider. One of four key knowledge-management functions. See *knowledge mapping*, *externalization*, *internalization*, and *cognition*.

Internal awareness – the first component of the knowledge-chain, which represents an organization's collective understanding of its strengths and weaknesses across structural silos and functional boundaries. Internal awareness is not only having your house in order, but also knowing what order your house is in. See *knowledge-chain*.

Internalization – the transfer of explicit knowledge from an external re-pository (temporary or permanent) to an individual, in the most useful and efficient way possible. There are two aspects to internalization: ex-traction and filtering. One of four key knowledge-management func-tions. See *knowledge mapping, externalization,* and *cognition.*

Internal responsiveness – the second component of the knowledge-chain, which represents an organization's ability to instantly organize skills based on an unfiltered assessment of its resources and external market demands and opportunities. See *knowledge-chain.*

KM$^{2\ TM}$ – the premier methodology for conducting a knowledge audit. KM^2 exposes and defines: an organization's propensity for knowledge man-agement; the value of knowledge; its ability and speed in traversing the knowledge cycle; and the current sources of knowledge. KM^2 analysis also uncovers pockets of deviance from the organizational norm, thereby identifying key opportunities that can be leveraged within the organiza-tion, and key obstacles that must be overcome.

KQML – the knowledge query and manipulation language, is a language and protocol for exchanging information and knowledge. It is part of the ARPA knowledge-sharing effort aimed at developing techniques and a methodology for building large-scale, sharable and reusable knowl-edge bases. KQML is a message-format and a message-handling proto-col to support run-time knowledge-sharing among agents. KQML can be used as a language through which an application program interacts with an intelligent system or through which two or more intelligent systems share knowledge in support of cooperative problem-solving. Information on KQML can be found on the world-wide-web at http://www.cs.umbc.edu/kqml/. [Definition taken from www.cs.umbc.edu.]

Knowledge-architect – see *knowledge leadership.*

Knowing enterprise – an enlightened organization that uses its instinct and accompanying self-awareness; an enterprise that has intimate, constantly renewed knowledge about itself, its capabilities, resources, and opportunities.

Knowledge-audit – an assessment of an organization's current achievements in knowledge management, its current knowledge-ecology, and the mapping of available tacit and explicit knowledge resources. See *KM²*.

Knowledge base – typically used to describe any collection of information that also includes contextual or experiential references to other metadata.

Knowledge-bazaar (info souk, etc.) – a form of knowledge-market in which sellers are essentially undifferentiated and buyers assume all quality and serviceability risks. See *knowledge-market.*

Knowledge-broker – a person, organization, or process which identifies intersections between knowledge-seekers (buyers) and knowledge-providers (sellers) and creates a vehicle for linking the two.

Knowledge-buyer – an individual that needs to access knowledge held by another individual or stored in a repository.

Knowledge-chain – corporate instinct, stemming from the flow of knowledge through four definitive stages in this chain: internal awareness, internal responsiveness, external awareness, and external responsiveness.

Knowledge-concierge – a title adopted by some organizations for individuals who have the responsibility of facilitating the transfer of knowledge across communities of practice. See *knowledge-broker*.

Knowledge-ecology – the component of knowledge management that focuses on human factors: namely, the study of personal work habits, values, and organizational culture.

Knowledge-engineer – see *knowledge-leadership*.

Knowledge-guild – a descriptive term for an organized group of suppliers of a specific kind of knowledge. Knowledge-guilds guarantee a level of quality in business interactions with their members. This guarantee differentiates guild members from others who might be active in "selling" similar knowledge in a *knowledge-bazaar*.

Knowledge half-life – the point at which the acquisition of new knowledge is more cost-effective and offers greater returns than the maintenance of existing knowledge.

Knowledge-leadership (types of) – a broad category of positions and responsibilities, from individuals who literally fall into the *de facto* position of knowledge-manager with no change in title, formal responsibilities or compensation to very well compensated senior executives who are recruited specifically for the role of the chief knowledge officer (CKO). Although no taxonomy could possibly set forth all of the titles and responsibilities included under knowledge-leadership, the following typify the general categories you are likely to encounter today:

- The *chief knowledge officer* is responsible for enterprise-wide coordination of all knowledge leadership. The CKO typically is chartered by the CEO and is often (but not always) part of it. The CKO's focus is the practice of knowledge leadership, usually solo performer role with no immediate lob responsibility. Before a culture of knowledge-sharing, incentives, and the basic precepts of knowledge leadership have been acknowledged by the enterprise, the CKO is powerless.
- The *knowledge-analyst* collects, organizes, and disseminates knowledge, usually on-demand. They provide knowledge leadership by becoming walking repositories of best practices, a library of how knowledge is and needs to be shared across an organization. There is a risk that these individuals become so valuable to their immediate constituency that they are not able to move laterally to other parts of the organization where their skills are equally needed.
- The *knowledge engineer* converts explicit knowledge to instructions and programs systems and codified applications. Effectively, the better knowledge-engineers codify knowledge, the harder it is for the organization to change when their environment demands it.
- The *knowledge manager* coordinates the efforts of engineers, architects, and analysts. The knowledge manager is most often required in large organizations where the number of discrete knowledge-sharing processes risk fragmentation and isolation. The risk in having knowledge managers is that fiefdoms (albeit large ones) may begin to form around the success of each manager's domain.
- The *knowledge steward* provides minimal, ongoing support to knowledge-users in the form of expertise in the tools, practices and methods of knowledge leadership. The steward is usually an individual who has fallen into the role of helping others better understand and leverage the power of new technologies and practices in managing

knowledge. The term "steward" seemed to resonate best among participants in the Delphi Group's knowledge-leadership study because it conveys responsibility and a willingness to guide others yet it is also non-intrusive and the near antithesis of ownership.

Knowledge management – the leveraging of collective wisdom to increase responsiveness and innovation.

Knowledge-manager – see *knowledge-leadership*.

Knowledge-mapping (knowledge-taxonomy) – a process which provides an organization with a picture of the specific knowledge it requires in order to support its business processes.

Knowledge market (knowledge bazaar, info souk, etc.) – an online gathering place where owners of intellectual property can barter, sell and otherwise exchange their intellectual property for value. Such markets may be undifferentiated, e.g. knowledge-bazaars; organized through knowledge-brokers; or modulated through the instrument of the knowledge-guild.

Knowledge-provider – an individual that possesses knowledge of value to other individuals.

Knowledge seeker – see *knowledge-buyer*.

Knowledge-seller – see *knowledge-provider*

Knowledge-steward – see *knowledge-leadership*.

Knowledge topology – a framework that segments knowledge management into four key categories: *intermediation, externalization, internalization,* and *cognition.*

Learning-organization – an organization with the necessary practices, culture, and systems to promote the continuous sharing of experience and lessons learned. Popularized by Senge. Knowledge-management systems seek to identify through knowledge-mapping, and to implement through competency management, the kinds of specific organizational and individual learning that must take place if the business is to build and maintain the required competencies to compete effectively.

Linguistic analysis – a form of concept-based retrieval in which semantic networks, lexicons and parsers are used to determine the overall subject matter of a body of text.

Matrix organization – the synthesis of central control and decentralization structures within a single organization. A matrix organization is typically organized around task forces or teams consisting of functional members.

Metadata – data providing context or otherwise describing information in order to make it more valuable as part of a knowledge-management system; most often used to connect information in relevant ways to people, process, or product.

Metaskills – the basic tool of generative learning; these skills are aimed at ensuring three things: skills-adaptability, autonomous decision-making, and an emotional aptitude for change.

Middle office – the role and function of knowledge workers who are positioned between front-office and back-office systems. This is the point where competitive differentiation is realized and where risk is minimized and profit maximized.

Organized abandonment – the process by which new innovations replace current products before the current product is out of its profit zone. See *profit zone.*

Overabundance (theory of) – the basis for creating a learning system. This theory postulates, "learning can only occur when the information provided from a transaction significantly exceeds the information required at no additional cost." In other words, diminishing cost of incremental information can result in increasing returns.

Perpetual organization – an organization that is without any permanent structure; it takes on whatever form is suitable for current conditions and market demands.

Personalization – retrieving and structuring knowledge to best meet the preferences and skills-set of the knowledge-seeker.

Process asset – a set of rules and instructions about a particular process set forth in a methodical and reusable manner.

Process-knowledge – the collection of tacit and explicit knowledge relating to the effective execution of a process. The creation of a process-asset that ultimately contributes to core competency must include the instinctive, tacit knowledge that contributes to the success of that process. This tacit knowledge can be reduced to a set of rules or converted to explicit knowledge and added to the knowledge base. This process-knowledge can then be managed more effectively and contribute to a living knowledge-chain of competitive assets which are easily modified as customers and markets change.

Profiling – the creation of chronicles that track user interest levels and areas of expertise. In an automated approach, profiles are created by monitoring each user's work submitted, work reviewed, and query habits. Profiling is used to feed agent-technology, user-sensitivity systems, and document-management systems.

Profit zone – the period of time during which a product's profitability is realized. Knowledge management should provide the practices and culture by which an organization can consistently maintain overlapping product cycles, thereby never falling out of the profit zone. See *organized abandonment*.

Response/stimuli matrix – a knowledge-management model which plots where memory and knowledge are best used. The matrix indicates that memory is an appropriate vehicle for responding in planned ways to anticipate stimuli. Knowledge is an appropriate vehicle for responding in unplanned ways to surprise stimuli.

Return-on-time (ROT) – a metric for assessing quickly if a knowledge-chain is working. Since instinct reduces the time required to go through this cycle, it increases a company's velocity and return-on-time. Specifically: $((P/100)*(sY/nY))$, where P = percent of profit, sY = sustained years, nY = number of years.

Semantic analysis (semiotics) – the analysis of meaning in text. In the context of knowledge-management software, a set of analysis programs which identify concepts in documents and their relative importance to the subject of the document and to each other. These utilities form the basis for accurate search and knowledge-discovery. See *concept-based search*.

Socialization – bringing together of individuals with similar interests. The purpose of communities of practice and communities of interest is to create a vehicle to promote the discovery and sustenance of tacit knowledge by encouraging socialization among individuals with similar knowledge and interests.

Solution-broker – a new class of solution-provider, offering a fully integrated solution for most business applications, integrating the component technology with the existing hardware infrastructure, significantly minimizing the risk factors associated with the technology integration.

Stimulus/response-opportunity matrix – a framework which identifies the relative opportunity for corporate portals in contrast to the current market for enterprise-transaction systems (ERP).

Structural capital – one of three forms of intellectual capital as defined by Edvinsson and Stewart; refers to the value, usually not reflected in accounting systems other than as goodwill, which results from products, systems, or services an organization has built. These may survive the absence of human capital for a period of time (i.e. the brand equity of a popular product), but will soon result in a core rigidity without the infusion of human capital. See *customer capital* and *human capital*.

Suggestive software – capable of deducing a user's knowledge-needs and suggesting knowledge-associations that the user cannot make.

Tacit knowledge – one of two types of knowledge; its taxonomy was most notably espoused by Michael Polanyi. Tacit knowledge is experiential know-how based on clues, hunches, instinct, and personal insights; distinct from formal, explicit knowledge.

Touch points – the priority areas for the application of knowledge management; typically interactions with customers, suppliers and with employees. Each touch point represents an area of potential process- or quality-improvement and competitive advantage. Touch points represent areas where human interaction is often most intense.

User sensitivity – the ability of an online system to track and manage the experience and preferences of a user, and to use this knowledge to tailor the delivery of knowledge to that user. Through user sensitivity approaches, the level of communication within a knowledge management system is heightened.

Velocity of innovation – the rate at which an organization is able to conceive of and introduce a new product to market. Innovation is driven by business markets that are battling against time to beat their competitors to the next product innovation. The automation of the innovation cycle and resulting decline in time to market is the 21st-century equivalent of the automation of production cycles in manufacturing during most of the 20th century. See *return on time* and *concept to cash*.

Virtual organization – a company "without walls" and without many permanent employees; it relies on contractual relationships with suppliers, distributors, and a contingent workforce.

Virtual team – a recombinant structure for work that pulls people and resources together quickly to solve a particular internal or external problem.

Visualization – the ability to visualize a process in intimate detail, capturing parameters about the process that can be used for interpretation, analysis, and discussion. Visualization ideally depicts the process and helps to analyze it. It creates a corporate memory of the process, provides data for analyzing the process, and creates a dynamic framework for a collaborative reengineering of the process.

Work-cell – a collection of roles within an organization that crosses functional barriers; individuals in these cells are distinguished by their flexibility and adaptability.

Workflow – one of the tools used for the creation of process-assets – a proactive toolset for the analysis, compression, and automation of business activities.

Index